Scrumdiddlyumptious

Delicious Multicultural recipes that is easy to cook.

"It's only 1 serving"

Ms. Luvenia Williams

DEDICATION

This book dedicated to the following people who encouraged me to be the best that I can be:

My Godmother, Willie Mae Hall (may she R.I.P).

My Grandmothers, Grandfathers (R.I.P).

My Niece, Luvenia Williams aka (Lil Lulu, R.I.P).

My Mentor, Mr. Gilbert Rose (R.I.P).

My Mother, Delores Williams-Burns (R.I.P).

My Father, Wilbur Williams II (R.I.P).

And a host of family and friends (R.I.P)

More information on this book can be found on Amazon, twitter, Facebook, and Pinterest

Printed and bound in the United States of America

ISBN # 9781089728559 (PAPERBACK)

Special thanks to Mr. Danny M from PS 001. (Public School Bronx, NY) for believing in me.

A little history about my mother

My mother was a person that had a challenging life in the early 60's-70's. She struggled while raising four children with the little money that welfare gave her. There was time she barely paid the rent, but she made it possible for her family to eat. I will hear her always thanking the lord for the food pantries and next-door neighbors that helped. We would probably have starved. Being a godly woman and having a spiritual soul. Her prayers and asking for help, made a way to feed her family, because jobs were scarce for black women during the sixties.

My mother was not that type of women who will roll over and die when times were hard. She was a proud woman with a wonderful heart that beats the sound of "Oh Happy Days". She had a great sense of humor, and never lost her confidence and dignity in spite of everything she went through. She taught her kids to always give, and have pride and dignity in ourselves.

Mama! We love you and miss you, please keep watching over us.

Contents

Acknowledgments

I am thankful for my wonderful family and friends: my dearly loved Mother Delores R. Williams-Burns; My dearly loved Dad Wilbur Williams Jr; My dearly loved Stepfather Nathaniel Burns; My loving Sister Desiree L. Williams-Henderson;My Brothers; Craig, Wilbur William; and Nathaniel Keith Burns. My Auntie Sonia and a host of cousins, uncles, nephews, nieces, and inlaws.

The Remarkable, Unforgettable teachers:

- **P.S. 123** In **Harlem NY**: Mrs. Williams suggested that I take up cooking.

- **Park West H.S NY:** The cooking teacher who had made a greatest impression on me was dearly loved Betty Sklaroff. She pushed me to enter in a Tri- State cooking contest in which I won First

Place.

- **Physical Education teacher:** I remember and honor Mr. Gilbert Rose. He who taught me how to play softball. He was my mentor, and a father figure to me.

- **College of New Rochelle:** Professor Aguilera: who planted these words of knowledge in me: "Do the best in life and don't let anyone tell you that you can't do it because you have the power?"

- **LaGuardia Community College**: Professor G. Angelakis: She is the greatest Professor of all in my opinion. Professor Angelakis always challenged me to expand my mind with possibilities so that I could achieve my goals.

- **Professional Helpers**: Mr. Hector V. Lino, registered teacher, and private tutor. He tutored me throughout the four years of College of New Rochelle. Mr. Lino, I thank you for the sacrifices you have made for me. You now have an impact on the way I look at life, and have contributed to the person I am today.

- **Ms. Roseann Shepherd:** Registered teacher, and private tutor who were always in my corner when I needed her. **Friends:** Dawn Part low (best friend, over 40 years of friendship), and a host of friends everywhere that are far too many.

- **A special thanks to Morella Bynoe.** She was by my side from the day I decided to return to college in 2007. When I needed her help with any assignment, she would take time out of her schedule to help me even though she was in college herself. I am grateful for her friendship, her ambition and dedication to make sure that I understand my assignments. Morella you are my role model. Thank you

I am acknowledging my mother's favorites recipes

- Mama's Fried Chicken
- Mama's Red Rice
- Mama's Baked Beans
- Mama's Cabbage with Turkey Meatballs
- Mama's Macaroni & Cheese
- Mama's Potatoes Salad
- Mama's Macaroni Salad
- Mama's homemade Corn Bread
- Mama's Smoke Neck bones & black eye peas
- Mama's Chicken Egg Noodle Soup
- Mama's Southern Gumbo
- Mama's Beaufort Stew
- Mama's Six seasoning Fried Fish (whiting)
- Mama's Salmon Cakes

Note: You will see Mama's in front of some recipes.

Introduction

About The *Cookbook*.

This *Cookbook* has multicultural recipes. From Moroccan, Jamaican, Soul food, Dominican, Greek, Cuban, Mediterranean, Indian and Spanish. With these recipes, I want a way for the readers to popularize remarkable single service size, and some helpful knowledge on cooking control. Like, temperatures, cooking danger-Zones, and be able to convert the recipes back to quantities service. In addition, I added hosts of tips, notes, safety tips, and add-in to help create a better dish, and to be safe while cooking.

In this *Cookbook*, I have converted some of my favorite recipes. In this endeavor, I took many of my family's staple, and my own created recipes and broke them down into a single serving size. Recipes service quantities, usually four to six. However, these recipes are only for one servicing. People can save money and stop wasting food when you cook the right portion. Any person can utilize this *Cookbook* to cook that quantities size dishes, and create wonderful and healthy food.

I always believed that, when it comes down to cooking, every person has such culinary talent, but some time needs a little push. This *Cookbook* shares a multitude of greatness to teach others that they can cook too. I would like to introduce one of my latest dishes: Hot Roasted Pineapple Shrimp with corn salad on rice cakes. You can serve these recipes for brunch or lunch with a cold glass of fruity raspberry ices tea.

Tip: Learn about EWG (Environmental WorkingGroup) http://www.ewg.org/foodscores

How to Store fruits & Vegetables

1.Apples	Stems in water for 3 days in refrigerator
2.Asparagus	Stems in water for 3 days in refrigerator
3.Avocados	Counter top to ripen then refrigerator for 3days once it is
4. Bananas	Counter top to ripen unwrapped for 3 days
5.Bell Peppers	Refrigerator for 7 days
6.Berries	Uncovered container and refrigerator for 4days
7. Broccoli	In plastic bag in refrigerator for 5 days
8. Cabbage	Refrigerator for 14 days
9.Cauliflower	Refrigerator for 5 days
10.Cucumbers	Refrigerator for 5 days
11.Carrots	Refrigerator for 21 days

12. Celery	Refrigerator for 14 days
13. Gingers	Refrigerator for 1 month
14. Grapes	Refrigerator in its own perforated bag 7 days
15. Lettuces	Refrigerator for 7 days
16. Melons	Counter top to ripen, after ripen 4 to 5 days
17. Mushrooms	Refrigerator for 3 days
18. Onions	Pantry for 1-2 months
19. Peaches	Counter top to ripen, after ripen 3 days
20. Pears	Counter top to ripen, after ripen 4 days
21. Plums	Counter top to ripen after ripen 5 days
22. Potatoes	Pantry for 1-2 months
23. Squash	Refrigerator for 5 days
24. Sweet potatoes	Pantry for 14 day
25. Tomatoes	Counter top to ripen, after ripen 5 days

26. Winter Squash	Pantry for 1 month

Tip: keeping all your vitamins and mineral in your veggie. It is best to steam them.

How to store your meats

Freezer (0 degrees)	Refrigerator
Bacon.... 3-12 months	6 days
Chicken.... 9-12 months	1-2 days
Pork Chops ....4-12 months	2-4 days
Crawfish...3-5 months	1-2 days
Fish...2-6 months	1-2 days
Ground meat...2-3 months	1-2 days
Livers...3-4 months	1-2 days
Lunch meats.... 1 months	2-3 days
Scallops.... 2-3 months	1-2 days
Shrimps.... 3-5 months	2-3 days
Steaks.... 5-12 months	3-5 days
Turkey.... 9-12 months	1-2 days

Safety tip: When thawing out meat or seafood. Thaw it out on the bottom of the refrigerator 1 to 2 days before. Make sure that there are NO food items on the same shelf, because you can have a major cross contamination problem if your meats or seafood is leaking liquid onto the food.

Cooking Techniques/Methods

Al dente- when you not overly soft pasta but still with a slight resistance.

Baking-when you cook by dry heat in the oven.

Barbecuing- when you slow direct heat cooking, as well as basting with a barbecue sauce in an oven or on a grill.

Blanching- When you pre-cooking or part cooking of food by dipping into boiling water.

Boiling- when you cooking of foods in a liquid bought to a boiling point of 212F

Braising- when you cook slowly in a small amount of liquid that keep the foods moist and add flavor. You have to keep the covered on the pot.

Deep-Frying- when you cook in a deep layer of hot fat.

Frying-when you cook in a large amount of hot fat.

Grilling- when you cook on a grill over extreme heat

Marinating-when you moisturize pieces of meat, poultry, seafood vegetable, or fruits by soaking them in a liquid mixture of seasonings.

Mise en Place- Get all ingredients together, "putting in place", as in set up.

Pan-frying-when you cook in insignificant amount of fat

Poach- when you cook very lightly in hot liquid just below the boiling point.

Roasting-when you cook by dry heat in an oven.

Sautéing- When you cook and brown food in a small amount of fats.

Sear- when you brown very quickly by intense heat.

Shocking-when you drop into ice water in order to stop the cooking. Such as vegetable or fruits that are commonly boiled in salted water and immediately shocked.

Simmering- when you boiling in moderately with gentle surface motion.

Steaming-when you use a small amount of water to make steam from a double boiler or kettle with a tight cover.

Stir-frying-when you quickly cook foods over high or medium-high heat in a lightly oiled skillet.

Tip: When you cooking, you have to rely on simple traditional cooking techniques and cooking equipment, most of them are measuring utensils.

Common Abbreviations
Equivalent Measurements

Conversions
8 pinches = 1 teaspoons
16 dashes = 1 teaspoons
60 drops = 1 teaspoons
1teaspoon = ½ Tablespoon
3teaspoons= 1 Tablespoon
2 tablespoons= 1 fluid ounces
2 tablespoons= 1/8 cups
4 tablespoons=1/4 cup or 2oz
51/3 tablespoons=1/3 cup
8 tablespoons=1/2 cup or 4 oz.
10 2/3 tablespoons=2/3 cup
12 tablespoons= 3/4 cup
16 tablespoons=1 cup or 8oz
8 fluid ounces=1 cup

2 cups=1 pint	
2 pints=1 quart	
4 cups=1 quart	
4 quarts=1 gallon	
C, c= cup	
Lb. = Pound	
Tsp. = teaspoon	
Tbsp. = Tablespoon	
Ea. = Each	

Tips On food handling safety

- Always wash your hands with soap and hot water to prevent cross contamination and germs.

- Wear a hair net, apron and gloves while handling raw food in the preparation area.

- Remember to thaw food on the bottom of the refrigerator.

- Cook all food thoroughly.

- "When in Doubt, throw it out" ...If the food DO NOT look or smell good.

- Make sure to sanitize the preparation area surface with one cap full of bleach to one gallon of water. Keep your food safe by keeping cold food cold on 40 degrees and below and hot food hot on 140 degrees and up. Food will not be safe if the temperature is in the danger zone 40 degrees to 140 degrees.

- Check dates at all time when buying products.

- Placing dates on your food can help you keep up with how long you have stored your food.

- When you sit cooked food out on the counter overnight. Bacteria cells can divide and grow every twenty minutes.

Getting ready for the lunch shift at Bowery Residents

Committee (BRC) where I volunteer on Sundays

Temperature Conversion

	Fahrenheit
Hot Oven	500-400
Moderate Oven	350-375
Low oven	300-250
Freezing point	0 -17
Water freezers	0- 32
Refrigerator cold point	32- 41
Boiling Point	212-up
Hard boiling	250-up
Danger Zone	40-139
Holding point	140-up
Cooking Point	165-up

The Claw Grip

First thing first is safety: ALWAYS! Keep your eyes on what you are doing and your surroundings before you commence to cutting anything. Make sure that you hold the knife correctly. Example: It is best to uses the hand you write with (righty or lefty), positioning your hand close to the blade so that your thumb is on one side and your pointed finger is curl back. When cutting, the tip of your knife stays on the cutting board at all time. While your opposite hand should be in the claw position to hold the food item. Then slide the knife slowly across the items.

Julienning- A stick-shaped cut which is thin as matchstick, measurement are 1/8 inches thick and 2 inches thick long.

Brunoisin-Cube-shaped cuts, measurements are 1/8inches thick cut.

Dicing/Cubes- Have three sizes example: Small dicing are cube shaped cuts measurements are ¼inches thick cut, medium dicing measurements are ½inches thick cut, and large dicing measurement are 3/4inches thick cut.

Mincing- you create a hand full of thin stripes, and begin to dice the food in very tiny bits.

Slice- Cut into thin slices.

Shredding- Tear or pull with a fork into shreds.

Peel-When you remove the outer skin.

Equipment and Utensils

Ramekin (5oz-9oz)	Stove
Spatulas, Metal, or rubber	Oven
Conventional oven	Convection ovens
Measuring cup (dry)	Refrigerator
Measuring cup (liquid)	Mixing bowl
Knives	Microwave
Sauté pan	Cutting board
Saucepan	Frying pans
Measuring spoons	Tongs
Pastry brush	Scale
Bread pan	Wooden spoons
Thermometer	Forks
Spoons	Peeler
Ladles	Colander
Whisk	Bowls-Small, Medium, and Large

Garlic presser	Food containers
Peppermill	Blender
Kitchen Timer	Salad spinner
Lemon presser	Slotted spoons
Can opener	Potatoes masher
Food Processor	Corkscrew

Tip: 5 oz. ramekins are just the right size for one person. However, you can use the 6-9oz too.

Notes

Appetizers

- Baked Pita Chips with Homemade Hummus
- Parmesan Hush Puppies
- Falafels
- Chicken Cheese Baguette
- Glazed Grilled Mini Chicken Sandwiches
- Onion Rings
- Onion Pancakes
- Crispy Seafood Pockets
- Country Fried Okra
- Sweet Potatoes Chips
- Turkey vegetable Wrap
- "**Hot** "Jerk Chicken Wings
- Coconut Curry Chicken Wings
- Fried Shrimp w/ Coconut Cream Sauce
- Mama's Fried Chicken
- Chicken Pot Pie
- Shepherd's Pie
- Sweet-Potato Fries w/ special sauce
- Baked eleven herds French Fries

- Mama's Salmon Cakes
- Toaster Oven Pizza
- Desi's Fish Stew/w Boiled Dumplings

Safety Note: You cannot leave food cooking unattended because it may cause a fire.

Baked pita chips with homemade

Hummus spread

Ingredients:

3oz Chickpeas, (rinsed)

1/2 Tbsp. Garlic in oil

1/4 c. Olive oil, (plus more for serving)

2 Tbsp. Fresh lemon juices

1 tsp. Ground cumin

1 tsp. Salt

Pinch. Black pepper

1 pk. Pita bread, (use 2 ea. pita)

Preparation:

Combine chickpeas, garlic in a food processor and blend for 1 minute; add olive oil, lemon juice, cumin, black pepper and salt and blend until smooth and creamy. Use 1 or 2 Tbsp. of water "if necessary to achieve the desired consistency". Transfer chickpeas hummus to a bowl. Drizzle it with olive oil before serving.

Pita Bread:

Preheat the oven to 350F.

Brush olive oil over each piece; cut the two-pita bread into 8 pieces; laid them onto a baking sheet pan and bake them until brown on each side. Once it done, set aside to cool. It is best to serve them warm.

Notes: These recipes measured for one service, but you can convert any amount of service if you like. Example; if you want to cook this recipe for 2, 3, or 4 people. The only thing you have to do is convert the amount into double, triple, or quadruple. If the original recipe call for ½ cup of flour and you cooking for two. Then you will use 1cup of flour.

Parmesan Hush Puppies

Ingredients:

1/4 c. All-purpose flour

1 oz. Grated Parmesan cheese, (fresh)

1/2 Onion, (finely chopped)

1/4 c. Yellow Corn meal

1/2 tsp. Brown sugar

1/2 tsp. Ground Cinnamon

1/4 tsp. Baking powder

1/4 c. Buttermilk, (use a little more as needed)

Pinch. Salt

1/8 tsp. Cayenne pepper

Pinch. Thyme, (dried)

1ea. Egg

1/2 c. Canola oil, (for pan-fry)

30 oz. Scoop

Preparation:

Place the cornmeal, brown sugar, cinnamon, flour, baking powder, thyme, cayenne, and salt in a bowl; mix with your hands. In another bowl, whisk together the egg, buttermilk, Parmesan cheese and onion and mix well. Pour wet ingredients into dry and fold until it all come together, the consistency should be thick. Heat the oil on medium- high; scoop mixture with a 30 oz. scoop and easy place into oil. Deep fryer or frying pan and cook until golden brown on both sides. Scoop it out and drain well on paper towel. Serve hot.

Tip: The recipe pairs very well with honey mustard sauce or Lulu's special sauce. Pg. 226

Falafel

Ingredients:

1/2 c. Garbanzo beans, (drained and wash)

1 tsp. Onion, (chopped)

1/2 Clove garlic, (chopped)

Pinch. Ground coriander

Pinch. Ground cumin

1ea. Egg

1 1/2 tsp. All-purpose Flour

Pinch. Salt

Pinch. White Pepper

1/2 c.Canola oil, (for frying)

30 oz. Scoop

1 Tbsp. Cucumbers, (diced)

1 Tbsp. Tomatoes, (diced)

Letters, (shredded)

1 ea. Pita bread

Preparation:

Place the chickpeas, garlic, onion, coriander, cumin, salt and white pepper in a food processor; mix for 1 minute until mixture is smooth; add the egg and mixed well. You want your result to be a thick paste consistency. Take mixture out of the processor into a bowl and add flour; mix well. Heat the oil on medium-high; scoop the mixture with a 30 oz. scoop and place easy into deep fryer or frying pan in oil and cook until golden brown on both sides. Set the falafel on paper towel to drain. Slice the top off the pita bread; stuff the falafel balls with shredded lettuce, cucumbers and tomatoes. Sever warm.

Tip: The recipe pairs very well with a drizzle of cucumber dressing, and a dash of hot sauce for better taste. Go to Pg. 204

Chicken Cheese Baguette

Ingredients:

4 sl. Baguette, (sliced and toasted)

2 oz. Cooked chicken, (boiled, white meat, chopped finely)

1/4 tsp. Garlic powder

Pinch. Salt

Pinch. Black pepper

1/4 tsp. Thyme, (dried)

1/4 tsp. Red peppers, (minced)

1/4 tsp. Green peppers, (minced)

1/4 c. Parmesan cheese, (grated)

Preparations:

In a pot, boil chicken for about 20 minutes or until chicken is tender. When done scoop out the chicken and set aside. In a bowl, add cooked chicken, salt, black pepper, thyme, red pepper and green pepper; mix well until everything is blended and set aside. Place the sliced baguette into a toaster oven or oven and brown on both side. Take a spoon and spread chicken mixture on sliced baguettes; sprinkle garlic powder and Parmesan cheese evenly, and then set back into oven

until cheese melted. Wait! Cool down a little then serve
warm.

Glazed Grilled Mini Chicken Sandwiches

Ingredients:

3 oz. Chicken breast, (Filet)

Pinch. Onion powder

Pinch. Garlic powder

Pinch. Thyme, (dried)

1 tsp. Brown sugar

1/8 tsp. Poultry seasoning

1 tsp. white wine vinegar

1 tsp. Worcestershire sauce

Pinch. Salt

Pinch. Black pepper

Olive Oil, (drizzle)

Pam Spray

1ea. Wheat Wraps

1ea. Leaf lettuce

1 Tbsp. Tomatoes, (sliced)

Preparation:

In a plastic bag place the brown sugar, garlic powder, poultry seasoning, thyme, onion powder, salt, and black pepper, vinegar, and Worcestershire mix well; add the chicken, squeeze out excess air, and seal the bag. Marinate overnight in the refrigerator.

Preheat the oven to 380F or George foreman grill on medium heat, then lightly oil or use Pam to spray the grill. Make sure to poke holes with a fork in the chicken. Cook chicken 5-7 minutes on both sides until lightly brown keep turning repeatedly until golden brown. Served with lettuce and tomatoes on mini wheat buns. Serve hot or cold

Tip: The recipe pairs very well with honey mustard sauce. Pg.224

Onion Rings

Ingredients:

1ea. Medium onion, (slice into ¼' rings)

½ c. All -purpose flour

3 tsp. Onion powder

Pinch. Salt

1 Tbsp. Sugar

Pinch. Cinnamon

1/4c. Skin 1% milk

1ea. Egg white

¼c. Water

3 Tbsp. Canola oil, (for frying)

Preparation:

Heat the oil in a frying pan. Separate the onion slices into rings. In a small bowl, stir together the flour, baking powder, sugar, cinnamon, and salt. Then you dip the onion slices into the flour mixture until they all coated.

Dip the floured rings into the batter, Batter; Whisk the egg and milk. Spread the breadcrumbs out on a plate or shallow dish. Place rings one at a time into the crumbs, and scoop the crumbs up over the ring to coat. Give it a hard tap as you remove it from the crumbs, Repeat with remaining rings. Fry the rings a few at a time until golden brown. Use paper towels to drain and serve with marinara sauce, special sauce or honey mustard sauce. Serve warm

Tip: The recipe pairs very well with salsa, or sweet and sour sauce.

Onion Pancakes

Ingredients:

1ea. Egg white

1/4 c. Water, (as needed)

1/4 tsp. Sesame oil

Pinch. Salt

1/2 c. Self- rise flour

1 tsp. Fresh cilantro, (finely chopped)

1Tbsp. Scallion, (finely chopped)

1 tsp. Toasted sesame seeds

2Tbsp.Canola oil, (for frying, or Pam spray)

Preparation:

Place the egg, water, sesame oil, and salt into a blender and blend well. Then add flour and blend until smooth, it should be the consistency lightly thick. Place the cilantro, scallion, and sesame seeds and mix well. Heat a nonstick skillet over medium high heat, and then place canola oil or spray the pan with pam. Pour in some of the batter, cook in sets. Flip the pancake with a spatula and cook on both sides until brown. Serve hot with the dipping hollandaise sauce.

Tip: The recipe pairs very well with the dipping hollandaise sauce. Pg.212

Notes: These recipes measured for one service, but you can convert any amount of service if you like. Example; if you want to cook this recipe for 2, 3, or 4 people. The only thing you have to do is convert the amount into double, triple, or quadruple. If the original recipe call for ½ cup of flour and you cooking for two. Then you will use 1cup of flour.

Crispy Seafood Pockets

Ingredients:

3ea. Large Fresh shrimp, (peeled, devein)

2oz. Tilapia fish, (chopped after cooked)

1 Tbsp. Shredded Colby cheese

1 tsp. Parsley flakes

Pinch. Cilantro, (fresh)

1ea Pastry rolls, (use only 2ea)

¼ tsp. Old bay seasoning

Pam spray

Preparation:

Pre-heat oven 375F.

In a sauté pan place shrimps and fish to cook until done. Then Place in a bowl mix shrimp, fish, cheese and parsley flakes, old bay seasoning and cilantro. Separate pastry dough. Place shrimp mixture into the center of one dough, then you press the other one to make a sandwich. After stuffing center, seal edges with tines of fork. Brush with egg. Spray Pam on cookie sheet and bake until golden brown. Serve hot or warm.

Tip: The recipe pairs very well with the dipping hollandaise, salsa, and cucumber sauce.

17

Country Fried Okra

Ingredients:

1/2 lb. Fresh okra, (5-8pieces, cut into ¼" thick)

1c. Canola Oil, (for frying)

¼ c. All-purpose flour

1ea. Egg white

1 tsp. Chili powder

Pinch. Ground rosemary

1tsp. Black pepper

Pinch. Salt

Pinch. Garlic powder

Preparation:

Beat egg with a wire whip or fork in a bowl and set aside; wash off okra and pour into bowl and mix until coated well with egg. Place flour, salt, black pepper, garlic powder, rosemary, and chili powder into another bowl and mix well. Remove the okra from the egg white mixture and dip it into flour mixture

Preheat frying pan on medium-high until hot then and add oil to coat bottom of pan. Shake off excess flour from okra then carefully add to the frying pan. Turn over and over, watching carefully so it does not burn on the bottom. When it is brown, take out of pan and drain on paper towels. Sprinkle with garlic salt and black pepper. Serve hot

Tip: to spice it up a little, sprinkle with jerk seasoning, Moroccan seasoning or sweet hot pepper sauce.

Sweet Potatoes Chips

Ingredients:

1ea Sweet potato, (sliced thin)

3/4 Tbsp. Canola oil (or Pam)

Pinch. Sea salt

Pinch. Cinnamon

Drizzles. Syrup

Pinch. Brown sugar

Pinch. Allspice

Preparation:

Preheat oven to 375F.

Clean and scrub, then dry the sweet potatoes, slice it as uniformly thin as possible. Make sure that you use a very sharp knife to get it uniformly thin.

Sprinkle a touch of allspice, and oil to lightly coat; lay the sweet potatoes chips on a baking sheet pan. Place the chip in the over, and then make sure you flip the chips after it is halfway cooked. Remove once crisp and brown. Let them rest for 5 minutes, drizzle syrup and Serve immediately.

Tip:recipe pairs very well with sprinkle sea salt, cinnamon, and brown sugar....Or you dipped the chip into Lulu's special sauce Pg.226

Turkey Vegetable Wrap

Ingredients:

1 tsp. Olive oil

1/4 lb. Deli Sliced Turkey Breast

1/2 Small green onions, (Julienne)

1oz. Watercress

1 Tbsp. Black olives, (sliced)

1 tsp. Fresh ginger, (finely minced)

1 tsp. Apple cider vinegar

1 tsp. Orange peels, (finely grated)

1ea. Green leaf lettuce

1/4 c. Bean sprouts

1/4 c. carrot, (grated)

1tsp. Fresh cilantro, (chopped)

2 tsp. Sweet chili sauce

1 ea. Wheat Wraps

Preparation:

Place the lettuce on the wheat wrap, then place a bit of turkey, onion, black olives, watercress, ginger, orange zest, and sprinkle the bean sprouts, carrots, apple cider vinegar, olive oil and cilantro. Roll the wrap neatly and cut in half. Serve cold

Tip: The recipe pairs very well with sweet chili sauce for dipping...You can also use other vegetables, tomatoes, cucumber, broccoli, spinach to put in wrap.

"Hot" Jerk Chicken Wings

Ingredients:

1/4 tsp. Garlic, (chopped Clove)

1/4 tsp. Ground allspice

1/4 tsp. Brown sugar

Pinch. Ground sage

1/2 tsp. Ground cayenne pepper

1/2 ea. Scotch bonnet peppers, (finely chopped)

1/2 tsp. Ground thyme

1 ea. Green onions, (chopped scallions)

Pinch. Ground cinnamon

1/4 tsp. White vinegar

1/4 tsp. Orange juice

Pinch. Ground nutmeg

1/4 tsp. Salt

1 tsp. Black pepper

1 tsp. Gravy master, (Brown)

1 Tbsp. Canola oil

1/4 lb. Chicken wings

Preparation:

Pre-heat oven 375 F.

In a blender, place all ingredients except chicken. Blend well. Place chicken in a food bag, add mixture, and coat well. Then let sit for 24 hours in the refrigerator. Next day place chicken in a casserole pan or you can place chicken on a grill. Make sure to shake off the extra mixture and set aside for brushing the chicken if necessary. Bake or grill until golden brown. Serve hot

Tip: The recipe pairs very well with Cole slaw. You can also use any parts of the chicken.

Coconut Curry Chicken Wings

Ingredients:

1/8 tsp. Ground curry powder

1/4 tsp. Ground turmeric

1/2 c. Lite coconut milk

1/4 lb. Chicken wings

Pinch. Salt

Pinch. Pepper

1 Tbsp. Canola oil

1 Tbsp. Olive oil

Pinch. Dill

Pinch. Parsley, (dried)

Preparation:

In a saucepan, heat 1-teaspoon olive oil, curry powder and cook on low heat about 1 minute, then place coconut milk, cook on low heat about 3minutes, and stir consistency.

Place the chicken in a bag; add salt and pepper, and turmeric. Shake well

In a frying pan, heat 1 Tbsp. of canola oil, and fry on each side until cook and thoroughly.

Reduce heat to medium, stir in the Coconut Curry Sauce, and simmer for 5 minutes. When done sprinkle the dill and parsley over the top. Serve hot

Fried Shrimp with Coconut Cream Sauce

Ingredients:

4ea. Large shrimp

1ea. Red-skin potatoes, (diced)

1/2 Tbsp. Onion, (chopped)

1 tsp. Olive oil

1/2 Tbsp. Canola oil

1 tsp. Ground curry powder Pinch. Turmeric

1ea. Garlic cloves, (minced)

1ea. Tomatoes, (diced)

1/4 c. Coconut milk

1/4 tsp. paprika

Pinch. Ground thyme

2 tsp. Scotch bonnet, (chopped finely)

Preparation:

For the Sauce: In a saucepan heat olive oil, combine, curry powder, turmeric, potatoes, onions, garlic, scotch bonnet and paprika. Cook on low heat. Then place coconut milk, thyme, and tomatoes cook on low heat until mixture well combined.

For the shrimps: Sauté shrimps on each side for 1 minute in canola oil until shrimp cooked well. Put the shrimps on plate and pour the sauce on top.

Tips: The recipe pairs very well over any style rice.

Notes: These recipes measured for one service, but you can convert any amount of service if you like. Example; if you want to cook this recipe for 2, 3, or 4 people. The only thing you have to do is convert the amount into double, triple, or quadruple. If the original recipe call for ½ cup of flour and you cooking for two. Then you will use 1cup of flour

Mama's Fried Chicken

Ingredients:

1ea. Wing

1ea. Breast

1/2 c. Buttermilk

1/2 c. All Purpose Flour

2Tbsp. Eleven herb seasoning, (look for seasoning recipe on page?)

1 tsp. Paprika

1Tbsp. Garlic powder

Pinch. Salt, (as needed)

1 tsp. Black pepper

1 c. Canola Oil, (for frying)

Preparations:

Place In a plastic bag, buttermilk and Chicken to marinated in the refrigerator for 2 hours. In a brown paper bag or in a bowl dredge chicken in flour, eleven seasoning, paprika and black pepper and mix well. Take chicken out of bag; shake off excess flour lightly and Place chicken in heated oil in a deep frying pan. Fry each piece until they are golden brown on each side.

Remove each piece of chicken and place on brown paper towel to drain the oil. The chicken can be served immediately or after it cool down a little.

Tip: The recipe pairs very well with Cole slaw or with potato salad, or lemony roasted asparagus and hot sauce.

Chicken Pot Pie

Ingredients:

1/2 Tbsp. Butter

1oz. Mushrooms, (diced)

Pinch Salt and pepper

1ea. White potatoes, (medium diced)

2oz. Celery (diced)

¼ c. Carrots, (medium diced)

2oz. Onion, (chopped)

¼ c. Peas

2 oz. Corn kernels

½ c. Heavy cream

2oz-3oz Chicken breast, (diced)

1/2 c. Chicken stock

Flaky pastry dough, (cut into discs)

Eggs wash (1 egg beaten into a bowl)

9oz. ramekin

Preparations:

Cook Chicken on medium heat with butter in a pan. Add mushrooms, potatoes, celery, onions, peas and corn and cook until tender. When vegetables are tender, lower the heat and add chicken stock and simmer until it begin to bubbles. Add the cream and simmer for 10 minutes.

Season with salt and pepper, place mixture into a 9oz ramekin, brush the edges of the ramekin with egg wash and cover the ramekin with the pie dough, Egg wash the top of the dough and make sure to poke holes for the steam to escape as the pie cooks. Bake at 375F until the top is golden brown. Set to the side to cool before eating.

Tips: Turkey Pot Pie—Substitute an equal amount of turkey for the chicken

Shepherd's Pie

Ingredients:

3oz Ground beef

1Tbsp. Green pepper, (chopped)

1Tbsp. Red peppers, (chopped)

1 ea. Fresh Garlic, (minced)

1/4 tsp. Ground cumin

Pinch. Salt

Pinch. Black pepper

Pinch. Thyme, (dried)

1 Tbsp. Tomato Paste

2 oz. Crushed Tomatoes, (used canned drain)

1/4 tsp Black pepper

1 Tbsp. Corn Nibble

1 Tbsp. Sweet peas

1 c. Mashed Potatoes, (1 large size whole potatoes or instants)

9 oz. Ramekin

Preparations:

In a sauté pan cook ground beef until brown. Make sure to discard fat. Add garlic, red and green peppers, corn, salt, black pepper, thyme, sweet peas and cumin. Cook 15 minutes on medium heat.

After cooking for 15 minutes add tomato paste, and crushed tomatoes to thicken the ground beef. In another pot make the instant mash potato or boil the whole potatoes until very soft. Mash potatoes, add cream and butter and whisk it until fluffy and set aside. After the beef mixture is nice and thick, place beef mixture into a 9oz thick ramekin. Then you place mash potatoes on top and spread it to cover beef mixture. Place the shepherd pie onto a baking sheet pan and into the oven to cook uncovered in 350 degrees for 10 minutes or until potatoes are golden brown. Serve Hot

Sweet Potatoes Fries with Special Sauce

Ingredients:

1 Tbsp. Olive oil

1/2 tsp. Chili-garlic sauce

1ea. Medium sweet potatoes (cut into thin slices)

Pinch. Ground cumin

Pinch. Chili powder

Pinch. Paprika

Pinch. Salt

Pinch. Ground black pepper

Pinch. Cinnamon

¼ tsp. Brown sugar

Pam Spray

Preparations:

Preheat oven to 425 degrees. Put sweet potatoes slices in a bowl whisk olive oil and toss to coat. Add cumin, chili powder, paprika, salt and pepper and toss again to coat. Arrange potatoes in layer on a baking sheet pan. Bake until golden brown, Turn potatoes and bake more minutes until golden brown on both sides. Remove potatoes from oven and serve with Lulu's special dipping sauce on (page 226)

Tip: This recipe pairs very well with cinnamon and brown sugar mixed and sprinkles over fries. Or dipping sauce

Baked Eleven Herds Baked Fries

Ingredients:

1ea. Large baking potatoes (cut into wedges strips, leave skin on)

1⁄4 tsp. Black pepper

1⁄2 tsp. Paprika

Pinch. Salt

2 tsp. Eleven herbs (see page 197)

1⁄2 tsp. Garlic powder

1Tbsp. Olive oil

Pam Spray

Preparations:

Preheat oven to 450F,

 Line a baking sheet with foil and spray with non-stick spray or olive oil. In a large bowl mix pepper, paprika, salt and garlic powder and the eleven herbs. Add the potatoes and olive oil and toss until well coated. Lay the potatoes on the baking sheet. Bake 10 minutes on both sides until golden brown and tender. Serve warm

Tip: The recipe pairs very well with Cole slaw and BBQ sauce or Lulu's special sauce.

Mama's Salmon Cakes

Ingredients:

3oz. Pink Salmon, (remove bones and liquid)

1ea. Egg

1 tsp. Onions, (chopped)

1/4 tsp. Green bell Pepper, (chopped)

1/4 tsp. Red bell pepper, (chopped)

Pinch. Salt

½ tsp. Old bay seasoning

1/4 tsp. Garlic Powder

1/2 tsp Black Pepper

½ c. Canola oil

1a. Wheat Bread (Cut in cubes)

1Tbsp. All-purpose Flour, (add as needed to adjust consistency)

Preparations:

In a bowl flake the salmon with a fork, add Egg, chopped Onions, Bell Peppers, Salt, Garlic Powder, old bay seasoning, Black Pepper, and the cubed bread. Mix the ingredients together. If the mixture is too moist, add a little flour as needed to adjust consistency.

Heat oil in frying pan on low heat. Scoop out the mixture with your hand, roll, and pat it into 2 patties then Set into the frying pan. Turn heat up to medium. Place the patties into pan and cook for 3 minutes on one side or until golden brown, turn the patties over and cook for another 3 minutes or until brown. When patties are brown on both sides, remove from pan and drain on paper towel. Serve while warm with Lulu's special sauce (page 226)

Tips: For more crunch on the outside, you might consider rolling the patties in cornmeal before frying. In addition, Lulu's special sauce. Pg 226

Toaster Oven Pizza

Ingredient:

1 ea. Naan tandoor flatbread

2ea. Heirloom tomatoes, (chopped finely)

1/4 tsp. Garlic powder

Pinch. Salt, (as needed)

Pinch. Black pepper

1 tsp. Italian blend spices

3/4c. Mozzarella cheese, (shredded)

1c. Water

1tsp. Fresh basil, (chopped or whole leaf)

Preparations:

In a small pot, bring water to a boiled. Take the tomatoes and set it into boiling water until you see the skin of the tomatoes start to peel, around 1 minute. Take tomatoes out and set into ice bath. Peel the skin off, then chop finely, and set aside.

In a sauté non-stick pan, add tomatoes, garlic powder, Italian spices, and black pepper. Cook until the mixture mixed well. If the mixture needs salt, then you add it. Take the naan bread and toast it on both sides. Keep naan bread on toaster tray. Then you spread tomatoes mixture onto bread until it is covered, then add basil on top. Sprinkle the mozzarella cheese over the sauce until it covered the sauce. Set the naan pizza back into the toaster oven and cook until the cheese melts. Serve hot. ***Tip: The recipe pairs very well with Green peppers and red peppers on top....Be careful eating the pizza. The sauce can be VERY HOT. Warning, wait until it cool down a little. Notes: These recipes measured for one service, but you can convert any amount of service if you like. Example; if you want to cook this recipe for 2, 3, or 4 people. The only thing you have to do is convert the amount into double, triple, or quadruple. If the original recipe call for ½ cup of flour and you cooking for two.***

Desi's Fish Stew with Boiled Dumplings

Ingredients:

3oz. Salt fish, (repeat boiling until the salt is off fish)

2 tsp. Garlic in oil

¼ of Green pepper, (Julianne)

1/4of Red pepper, (Julianne)

1 ea. Heirloom tomatoes, (Diced)

½ of Yellow onions, (Julianne)

1 tsp. Sofrito

1 Tbsp. Apple cider vinegar

1-1/2 tsp. Canola oil

1/8 tsp. Black pepper

Pinch. Cayenne pepper

Preparations:

In a pot add cold water on high heat, add salty fish with apple cider vinegar and boil for 20 minutes; pour off the water then add more cold water and boil again until there are no more salty taste; set aside. Put oil in a sauté pan on medium heat. Add garlic until golden brown; add green pepper, red pepper, cayenne pepper, onions, and fish. Let the vegetable sweat a little and frequently stir. Add diced tomatoes and sofrito mix well. Cook for 10 minutes, remove from heat and set aside. Serve it hot.

Boiled Dumplings:

Ingredients:

5 Tbsp. All-purpose flour

1/3 c. Water

Pinch. Salt

Preparations:

In a pot of water half-full, add salt and heat until water comes to a boil. While the water is boiling. In a bowl, add flour a water until it form into dough. If the dough is too wet, add a little more flour until the dough is no longer sticky. You knead the dough at least 5 -7 time; pick off a piece of dough and roll it in the palm of your hand. You stretch it out until you form a circle. Repeat with the rest of the dough; add dough into boiling water and cook for 20-30 minutes. Frequently stir lightly until done. Remove pot from heat, take out dumpling, and place it into bowl. Serve hot.

Tip: This recipes pair very well together pea and rice, and plantains. You can place stew over rice.

Notes

SOUPS

- French Onion Soup
- Lulu's Hookup soup
- Tomatoes Soup
- Mama's Chicken Egg Noodles Soup
- Wonton Soup
- " Hot" Pepper Pot Soup
- Vegetable Barley Soup
- Italian Fish Soup
- Moroccan Lentil and Chickpea Soup
- Homemade Chicken Vegetable Soup
- Mama's Beaufort Stew
- Egg Drop Soup
- Chicken and Bok Choy Soup
- Blackeyes pea Soup With Salt Pork
- Irish Lamb Stew
- Thai Hot Ass Soup
- Turkey and Orzo Soup
- Spicy Lamb Chili Soup
- Mondongo Soup
- Beef Stew

Tips: Food Borne Illness Link. This link is an excellent resource

http://www.cdc.gov/foodsafety/diseases

Notes

French Onion Soup

Ingredients:

¼ c. Beef broth

¼ c. Beef consommé, (see page 209)

½ c. Onions, (sliced ¼ 'thick rings)

½ Tbsp. butter

1tsp. Garlic cloves, (chopped)

Dash. Worcestershire sauce

1tsp.Swiss cheese, (shredded)

1 tsp. Monterey jack cheese, (shredded)

1ea. French bread, (toasted, small slices)

Pinch. Salt

Pinch. White pepper

1ea. Ramekin 9oz

Preparations:

Preheat oven 380F

Heat saucepan with butter and place onions, cook on low heat until onions are tender. Then add garlic, white pepper, salt and cook until tender for 2-3 minutes. Do not let garlic get too brown. Add beef broth, consommé, and Worcestershire sauce. Bring to a boil. Use a 5oz or 6oz ramekin and place the Monterey jack cheese in bottom of ramekin, Fill ramekin-leaving room at the top. Place toasted French bread on top and add Swiss cheese too. Place in preheated oven until cheese is melts. Serve hot.

Safety tip: WARNING--bowls will be hot! Wait until it cools down.

Notes: These recipes measured for one service, but you can convert any amount of service if you like. Example; if you want to cook this recipe for 2, 3, or 4 people. The only thing you have to do is convert the amount into double, triple, or quadruple. If the original recipe call for ½ cup of flour and you cooking for two. Then you will use 1cup of flour.

Lulu's Hook-up Soup

Ingredients:

3 oz Smoked neck bones

5 ea. Fingerling potatoes medley, (cut in halves)

1 Tbsp. Sweet corn, (canned)

1 Tbsp. Black eye peas, (dried)

1 Tbsp. Pearly onion

1/3 ea. Green pepper, (julienned)

1/3 ea. Red pepper, (julienned)

Pinch. Salt, (optional)

1 tsp. White pepper

¼ tsp. Thyme, (dried)

2 oz. Polish sausage, (cut in ¼ inches)

Pot of water.

1 ea. Cube of vegetable seasoning

5 ea. Carrots, (baby)

½ tsp. Kidney beans, (dried)

½ tsp. Lima beans, (dried)

Preparations:

In a medium pot of water, add neck bones. Cook for

11/2 hour on medium heat. Continue to add more water

as needed. Then add black eye peas, kidney beans, potatoes medley and lima beans. Cook for another 1 hour on medium heat.

Note: You have to keep your eyes on the pot because the water will evaporate time to time so that you can add more water.

Then you add a cube of vegetable seasoning, onions, green peppers, red peppers, white pepper, thyme and polish sausages. Cook for another 25 minutes and stir very slowly until the beans and potatoes are tender. Check if soup needs salt, and then add salt. This dish should have plenty of broth to be soup like. Serve hot.

Tip: This recipe pairs very well with buttermilk biscuits see recipe on Pg 181. Add-in: pigtails or pig ears, pig feet, cow feet. If you want to add some heat, add Jessie hot pepper dust, or scotch bonnet.

Tomatoes Soup

Ingredients:

3 ea. Diced tomatoes, (Heirloom, place in boiling water for 1 minute. Peel and dice)

½ tsp. Basil, (chopped fresh)

1 tsp. Oregano, (chopped fresh)

1 tsp. Fresh garlic, (minced)

¼ Tbsp. butter

½ Tbsp. Red onion, (finely chopped)

1 Tbsp. All-purpose flour

½ c. Chicken broth

½ Tbsp. Grated Parmesan cheese

Preparations:

Take the tomatoes and place in blender until pureed. In a saucepan, heat butter over medium-high heat and add onion, garlic, basil, and oregano. Cook until tender. Remove from the heat and set aside.

Take the flour and put it in a cup, then add a little cold water and stir until smooth. Place the tomatoes mixture into the saucepan and gradually whisk in the flour, and add broth, and cheese. Simmer over very low heat for

10 minutes, stirring occasionally, allow flavors to blend, strain soup through a colander. Serve hot

Tip: This recipe pairs very well with an open grill cheese sandwiches.

Mama's Chicken Egg Noodles Soup

Ingredients:

1ea. Chicken breast, (cubes)

1c. Chicken broth

1Tbsp. Carrots, (diced)

1Tbsp. Celery, (diced)

1 tsp. Onions, (diced)

Pinch. Black pepper

Pinch. Salt

1 tsp. Fresh parsley, (chopped)

Pinch. Thyme, (dried)

½ ea. Bay leaf

½ Tbsp. Butter

½ c. Egg noodles

½ c. Water

Preparations:

Combine the chicken and chicken broth in a stockpot and cook it over high heat until it comes to a boil, add carrots, celery, onions, garlic, salt, parsley, thyme, bay leaf, and water. Reduce heat and cook until the chicken is very tender. Skimming the surface of any fat. Add eggs noodle, butter, and continual cooking until noodles are fluffy and tender. Serve hot.

Tip: **This recipe pairs very well with oyster cracker or saltine crackers**

Wonton Soup

Ingredients:

Pinch. Thyme, (dried)

Pinch. Rosemary, (dried)

½ c. Chicken stock, (canned broth)

½ c. water

¼ tsp. Cornstarch

1 tsp. Scallion, (minced)

¼ lb. Ground chicken

1 stalk Celery, (julienne)

½ Tbsp. Carrots, (Diced)

1 tsp. Soy sauce

½ tsp. Sesame oil

Pinch. Sugar, (brown)

6 ea. Wonton wrappers, (Small size)

Preparation:

Soup:

Add scallions, soy sauce, water, sesame oil, thyme, rosemary and sugar into a large soup pot under low heat until it comes to a boil. Once boiled, reduce heat to very low, cover pot, and cook for 15 minutes then place pot aside.

Wontons:

Cook the ground chicken in a saucepan for 5 minutes on medium heat and stirring occasionally until done. Make sure you have a plate set aside. Fold the wrapper in half so that it looks like a triangle. Dip your finger into the water to moisten the edges of the wrapper. Place about 1 tsp. of the meat mixture in the center of the wrapper and fold in half to make a triangle. Press firmly with a fork along the edges to seal them. Repeat until you have all 6 of them made. The mixture you have set aside. Add chicken carrots, celery and put wonton into the broth to a boil. Reduce heat to low and cook for 5-7 minutes. Stir occasionally until wontons are firm and cooked through. Serve hot in a bowl

Tips: **You can add spinach leaves, or bokchoy and cook for 20 seconds until they done. Addon, Chinese noodles, French-fried onions, or cubes bread stuffing**

"Hot" Pepper Pot Soup

Ingredients:

1Tbsp. Tomatoes, (heirlooms, diced)

1 tsp. Green chilies

1 stalk. Scallion (cut in pieces)

1 Tbsp. Kernel corn, (can, drained)

½ tsp. Black beans, (can, rinsed and drained)

½ ea. Scotch bonnet, (minces)

1 Tbsp. Lima beans, (can and drained)

3oz. Beef, (cubed)

1 oz. Pigtails, (cut in halves)

1 oz. Lamb, (cubes)

1c. Beef stock

¼ tsp. Fish sauce

1 tsp. Mushrooms, (slices)

1 Tbsp. Okra, (cut into pieces)

1ea. Corn, (cob, cut in half)

Pinch. Salt

Pinch. Black pepper

Pinch. Thyme, (dried)

1 ea. Bay leaf

Preparation:

In a large stockpot, add beef stock, pigtail, lamb, corn on the cob, salt, black pepper, bay leaf, thyme and beef to a boil on medium heat or until meat is tender. Stir in the diced tomatoes, corn, black beans, lima beans and cook for about 5 minutes on low heat. Mix in the mushrooms stirring occasionally. Add the fish sauce; scotch bonnet and green chili pepper. Continue cooking until well blended. Add okra, and cook for 2 minutes. Remove from heat, and serve hot with buttermilk biscuits.

Safety notes: WARNING! The scotch bonnets are very hot. Make sure to wear gloves and DO NOT rub your eyes with the gloves.

Vegetable Barley Soup

Ingredients:

½ c. Pearl barley

1 c. Vegetable stock (or chicken stock)

1 tsp. Canola oil

½ c. Onions, (chopped)

¼ c. Carrot, (chopped)

1 Tbsp. Celery, (chopped)

2 tsp. Mushroom, (small sliced)

1 Tbsp. Tomatoes, (heirloom Diced, skin peeled)

Pinch. Salt

½ Tbsp. Fresh parsley, (chopped)

Preparations:

Place the tomatoes and ½-cup vegetable stock in a small pot and bring to a boil over medium-low heat, cover pan and simmer for 1/2 hour. In a sauté pan heat the olive oil and add the onion, carrots, celery, and mushrooms. Cook until the vegetables begin to soften. Add the remaining ½ cup vegetables stock and the barley, cover and simmer 10 minutes on low heat. Add salt to taste and scoop into a bowls. Serve hot and garnished with chopped fresh parsley.

Safety food Tips: Always wash your hands after using the bathroom, coughing, and sneezing, eating, washing the counters, handling raw meats, trash and dirty equipment, during food preparation.

Tips: Research Link:http://www.handle-foodsafely. A need to know.

Notes: These recipes measured for one service, but you can convert any amount of service if you like. Example; if you want to cook this recipe for 2, 3, or 4 people. The only thing you have to do is convert the amount into double, triple, or quadruple. If the original recipe call for ½ cup of flour and you cooking for two. Then you will use 1cup of flour

Italian Fish Soup

Ingredients:

3oz Tilapia, (fresh or frozen)

2 Large shrimps, (peeled and deveined)

1c. water

2 tsp. Tomatoes, (diced)

½ Tbsp. Carrot, (shredded)

1tsp. Celery, (chopped)

1 tsp. Apple cider vinegar

1 tsp. Chicken stock

½ tsp. Orange juice

1 tsp. Garlic cloves, (minced)

1ea. Bay leaves

1 Tbsp. Poblano peppers

1tsp. Tomato paste

1 tsp. Fresh oregano

Preparations:

Before making the soup, make sure to take out the fish and shrimps to thaw out in the bottom of the refrigerator, one day before if frozen. When thaw out, rinse fish and shrimp; pat dry with paper towels very good. Now! You have to cut the fish into squares and the shrimps in half.

In saucepan place water, celery, oregano, carrots, diced tomatoes, apple vinegar, chicken stock, poblano peppers, orange juice, garlic, bay leaves. Cook on high heat until it comes to a boil, then reduce heat low, cover and simmer until vegetables are nearly tender. Then stir in tomato paste and add the fish and shrimps. Continual to simmer more until fish flakes, check with a fork. Remove bay leaves. Serve hot immediately.

Tip: The soup pairs very well with toasted Italian bread. WARNING! The Poblano is very hot. Make sure to wear gloves and DO NOT rub your eyes with the gloves.

Moroccan Lentil and Chickpea Soup

Ingredients:

1ea. Onion

1 Tbsp. Butter

1tsp. Celery, (chopped)

Pinch. Ground cinnamon

Pinch. Ground turmeric

Pinch. Salt

½ tsp. Black pepper

Pinch. Ground ginger

¼ tsp. Scotch bonnet

¼ c. Tomatoes, (Diced pureed)

1/2c. Lentils

2 Tbsp. Chickpeas

½ c. Beef consommé (Pg. 209)

½ c. Orzo, (pasta)

1 Tbsp. Roux agent, (pg. 208)

½ Tbsp. Fresh parsley, (chopped)

¼ Tbsp. Fresh cilantro, (chopped)

2Tbsp. Lemon juice

Preparations:

In saucepan, melt butter over low heat. Combine onion; scotch bonnet, celery, and cook until onion is tender, stirring occasionally. Then you add the cinnamon, turmeric, salt, black pepper, and ginger. Continual cooking, stirring, for about 3 minutes. Then add tomatoes, lentils, chickpeas and broth. Bring to boil, and reduce the heat to low and simmer. Cook until lentils are tender.

Stir in the pasta and simmer on low heat, covered and wait until pasta is al dente. Whisk in roux into soup and simmer, and keep stirring until soup thickened, if not thickened continual to use more roux. Add in parsley, cilantro, and lemon juice. Serve hot

Tip: **The soup pairs very well with toast and grated fresh jben cheese on top of soup.WARNING! The scotch bonnet is very hot. Make sure to wear gloves and DO NOT rub your eyes with the gloves**.

Homemade Chicken Vegetables Soup

Ingredients:

3oz. Chicken Breast, (Cubes)

1tsp. Onion, (chopped)

1ea. Fresh garlic, (minced)

1ea. Basil, (dried)

¼ c. Tomatoes, (can crushed)

1c. Chicken stock (or veloute sauce Pg. 211)

1 Tbsp. Corn, (can)

1 Tbsp. Green lima beans (Can)

1 Tbsp. Carrots, (raw diced)

1 Tbsp. Black beans (can)

1 Tbsp. Green beans (can)

1 tsp. Black pepper

Pinch. Salt, (Use more if needed)

1 tsp. canola oil

Preparation:

In a stockpot, sauté chicken, onion, basil, and garlic in canola oil until tender. Then you stir in tomatoes, and chicken stock, (or veloute sauce pg. 211) and cook on high heat until it comes to a boil. Then add corn, salt, black pepper, green beans, black beans, carrots, and lima beans. Cook on low heat for about 20 minutes. In addition, serve hot

Tip: The soup pairs very well with toasted naan bread, cut into 4 triangles pieces, and garnish with cheddar cheese.

Mama's Beaufort Stew

Ingredients:

4 ea. Large shrimp, (unpeeled)

2 ea. Crawfish

1ea. Ears of corn, (frozen, cut in half)

½ ea. Kielbasa sausage (cut in pieces)

2 Tbsp. Old bay seasoning, (use more if needed)

2 ea. Small red potatoes, (unpeeled and cut in 4)

2 ea. Live crabs

4ea. Mussels

2ea. Little neck clams

Pinch. Salt

½ tsp. Cayenne pepper

1 tsp. Black pepper

1 ea. Bay leaf

Water, (half pot)

Preparations:

In a small stockpot, add salt, peppers, and bay leaf and half-full it with water. Add sausage, old bay seasoning, and ear of corn, crabs, clams, and mussels. Bring it to a boil, lower heat and add potatoes. Continual cooking until potatoes are tender. Add the shrimp, cooking just until the shrimp turn pink. Remove pot from heat and immediately drain pot and spoon mixture into large bowls. Serve hot

Tip: **The soup pairs very well with saltine crackers and plenty of paper towels. For an extra kick, add some jalapeno, or scotch bonnet, or Carolina reapers, or sprinkle some Jesse's Hot Pepper Dusk or just hot sauce. WARNING! The Hot peppers are very hot. Make sure to wear gloves and DO NOT rub your eyes with the gloves**.

Egg Drop Soup

Ingredients:

1c. Beef consommé, (or chicken broth, vegetable broth)

1ea. Egg, (beaten)

1 Tbsp. Scallion, (finely chopped)

Pinch. Salt

Pinch. White pepper

Pinch. Cayenne

Preparations:

In a small saucepot, bring consommé, cayenne pepper, salt, white pepper, to a boil. Whisk in beaten egg. Cook for 1 more minutes. Then add scallions and serve hot.

Tip: **The soup pairs very well with soy sauce to taste, finely sliced celery, and grated carrots. However, you have to cook the vegetable before you add the egg.**

Chicken and Bok Choy Soup

Ingredients:

½ ea. Onion, (sliced)

1ea. Fresh garlic, (sliced)

1 Tbsp. Canola oil

2oz. Chicken breasts, (sliced)

1c. Chicken stock

Pinch. Salt

Pinch. Black Pepper

1tsp. soy sauce

3oz. Baby bokchoy, (sliced)

1ea. Bay leaf

½ c. Orzo, (pasta)

2Tbsp. Carrots, (sliced thin)

Preparations:

In a sauté pan fry, cook all the vegetables carrots, garlic and onions until tender in canola oil, then set aside. In a small pot fill it with chicken stock, add the orzo pasta, bay leaf and cook until al dente. Cook the chicken and stir until brown. Add a pinch of salt, black pepper and the soy sauce and then add chicken with vegetable mixture and orzo pasta into the chicken stock. Use more stock if needed. Twist the leaves off the Bok Choy then add to the soup. Simmer for 20 minutes. Serve hot.

Tip: **This recipe pairs very well with more vegetables, chicken, turkey or lamb.**

Blackeyes pea Soup with salt pork

Ingredients:

1c. Black-eyed peas, (frozen)

2oz. Salty pork, (fat-back)

1Tbsp. Onion, (chopped)

1Tbsp. Celery, (diced)

1ea. Fresh garlic, (minced)

¼ c. Chicken broth

Pinch. Salt, (as needed)

Pinch. Black pepper

Preparations:

Boil the salt off the salty pork. Then fry the salty pork and then set aside the fat. Cook onion, celery and garlic in salty pork fat until tender. Add chicken broth, black pepper and black eyes peas. Bring to a boil and skim the top of the pot if necessary. Lower the heat to simmer. Cut the salty pork into cubes and add to peas. Cover and simmer until peas are tender. Used more stock if needed. Serve hot

Notes: These recipes measured for one service, but you can convert any amount of service if you like. Example; if you want to cook this recipe for 2, 3, or 4 people. The only thing you have to do is convert the amount into double, triple, or quadruple. If the original recipe call for ½ cup of flour and you cooking for two. Then you will use 1cup of flour

Irish Lamb Stew

Ingredients:

2 ea. Potatoes, (peeled and halved)

1ea. Fresh garlic, (minced

¼ c. Dry red wine

½ tsp. Irish whiskey

½ ea. Bay leaves

Pinch. Basil (dried)

Pinch. Salt

¼ tsp. Black pepper

¼ tsp. Thyme, (dried)

1 tsp. Dill, (fresh)

3oz. Lamb, (cubes)

1Tbsp.Olive oil

1c.Beef broth

2Tbsp. Carrots, (raw cut slices)

1Tbsp. Onions, (white)

Preparations:

In a dish shallow pan, combine all vegetables potatoes, garlic, carrots, bay leaf, thyme, red wine, salt, black pepper, basil and onion pour over meat. Cover and refrigerate for 24 hours. Drain the meat and reserve marinade sauce. Throw away the bay leaves. Heat oil in a pan over medium heat and brown the meat in oil until tender. Add beef broth and reserved marinade, bring to a boil, Cover and reduce heat, and simmer about 1 hour. Add the vegetable mixture cover and cook for 15minutes. Before serving add the whiskey, dill and serve hot.

Thai "Hot" Ass Soup

Ingredients:

1c. Chicken stock

1ea. Lemongrass (cut in 1-inch lengths)

½ ea.Lime leaves

Pinch Lime zest

½ ea. Serrano pepper (chopped)

2oz. Chicken breast, (cubed)

1oz. Shrimp, (devein)

2 Tbsp. Coconut milk

½ ea. Scotch bonnet (chopped)

¼ tsp.Fresh cilantro, (chopped)

1tsp. Onions, (chopped)

½ c of orzo pasta

Preparations:

Cook the chicken and chicken stock in a large pot with the lemongrass, lime leaves, lime zest, Serrano pepper, and scotch bonnet pepper. Bring to a boil, then cover, reduce the heat to low and simmer for 30 minutes. Then you add the shrimps until it done. Turn off the heat and add the coconut milk. Stir and mix well. Pour soup into bowls and sprinkle the cilantro and onions on top. Serve hot

Tip: **WARNING! The peppers are very hot. Make sure to wear gloves and DO NOT rub your eyes with the gloves.**

Turkey Orzo Soup

Ingredients:

3oz Turkey wing, (cut into pieces)

Pinch. Ground cumin

1/4 tsp. Ground oregano, (dried)

1/4 tsp. Ground black pepper

Pinch. Salt

1tsp. Onion, (white diced)

1 Tbsp. Carrots, (raw diced)

1/2ea. Poblano peppers, (diced) optional

1ea. Heirloom tomatoes, (diced)

1 c. Chicken broth

1/2c. Orzo, (pasta)

1Tbsp.Lime juice

1/2 tsp. Jalapeno, (minced) optional

1 tsp. Fresh cilantro, (chopped)

Preparations:

Place turkey in pot with broth, cumin, oregano, black pepper and salt under medium heat mix gently until tender. Add onion and carrots and cook on low heat, stirring often, until vegetables beginning to soften. Add, poblano and jalapeno peppers (hot peppers), lime juice and tomatoes and cook, keep stirring until soup mixed well. Add the orzo and cook, stirring occasionally until tender. Remove from the heat and serve hot. Garnish with cilantro.

*Tip:*WARNING! The Hot peppers are very hot. Make sure to wear gloves and DO NOT rub your eyes with the gloves.

Spicy Lamb Chili Soup

Ingredients:

1/2 ea. Bay leaf

Pinch. Salt

Pinch. Black pepper

1/2 Tbsp. onion, (diced)

3oz. Lamb chop, (cubes, deboned)

1tsp. Fresh garlic, (minced)

Pinch. Red pepper flakes

1/4 tsp. Oregano, (dried)

Pinch. Ground allspice

1/2ea. Jalapeno, (chopped)

1 Tbsp. Ground chili powder

1/2c. Tomatoes, (can diced with juice)

2Tbsp. Red beans, (can, drain)

1Tsp. Canola oil

1 tsp. Cilantro

1 tsp. Parmesan cheese

Preparations:

In a frying pan, coat pan with oil and heat. Cook lamb over medium heat until brown and tender. Then add onions, garlic, red pepper flakes, oregano, allspice, chili powder, bay leaf, and salt, jalapeno and black pepper. Sauté until vegetable are soften. Add tomatoes and beans mix well and bring soup to a boil. Then reduce heat and cook until soup ingredients all mixed well. Serve hot

Tip: **Garnish with toppings of cilantro and parmesan cheese.WARNING! The Hot peppers are very hot. Make sure to wear gloves and DO NOT rub your eyes with the gloves**.

Mondongo Soup

Ingredients:

3c. Water

1oz. Tripe, (wash well cut wide strips)

2oz. Cow feet

1Tsp. Salt

1 canola oil

1/2c. Tomato sauce

1 Tbsp. Potatoes, (diced)

1 Tbsp. Yucca, (diced)

1 Tbsp. Pumpkin, (diced, peeled)

1/2ea. Bay leaves

1ea. Clove garlic, (chopper)

Pinch. Black pepper

1Tbsp. White beans (can and drained)

1 Tbsp. Pearly Onion

1/4 tsp. Cilantro

Pinch. Ground coriander

1/4 tsp. Sofrito

1/8 tsp. Ground annatto

<u>Preparations</u>:

In a medium soup pot, add water, salt, black pepper, cow feet and tripe. Bring it to a boil on high heat. Lower the heat and cover. Simmer until the tripe and cow feet are tender about 2 ½ hours. Drain and take out of pot then rinse; set tripe and cow feet aside. Heat the oils in pot, add tomato sauce, potatoes, yucca, pumpkin, bay leaf, onions, sofrito, garlic, coriander, tripe, cow feet and annatto, Sautee over medium heat, add more cold water to cover mixture; reduce the heat, and simmer until the everything are cooked. Last thing is to add drained canned of white beans and simmer for 10 minutes before serving .Serve hot

Tip: Garnish with cilantro

Beef Stew

Ingredients:

3oz. Chuck roast beef, (cubes, and trim fat if necessary)

1 Tbsp. All-purpose flour

Pinch. Paprika

Pinch. Ground chili powder

Pinch. Fresh parsley, (chopped)

Pinch. Garlic powder

1/4 tsp. Salt

1 Tbsp. Canola oil

1/4 tsp. Onions, (diced)

3 Tbsp. Tomatoes, (can diced with juice)

1/2ea. Bay leaf

1c. Beef broth

1/2 tsp. Ground cayenne

1 Tbsp. Carrots, (raw, sliced ¼" thick)

1ea. Red potatoes, (peeled, cubed)

1 Tbsp. Parsnip, (peeled and diced)

2 Tbsp. Corn, (can, drained)

1 Tbsp. Green beans, (can, drained)

1/2c. Cold water, (if needed)

1Tbsp. Celery, (chopped finely)

Preparations:

In a bag, combine beef, flour, paprika, cayenne pepper, chili powder, garlic powder, and salt. Shake until the entire beef coat. In a frying pan, heat oil and brown meat over medium heat until brown.

Transfer beef into a soup pot, add water, bay leaf, beef broth, onions, and diced tomatoes, cover, and simmer until meat is tender. Then add carrots, potatoes, parsnip, celery and corn and simmer until tender. Add more water if needed. Add green beans at the last minute before serving; cook for 5 minutes. Serve hot and sprinkle parsley on top.

Tip: **If you like it thick, just mix 1-2 Tbsp. cornstarch with equal amount of cold water together. Then stir into pot while simmering to thicken. You also can add or sub peas for green beans. This recipe is well pair with corn bread and white rice or brown rice.**

Notes: **These recipes measured for one service, but you can convert any amount of service if you like. Example; if you want to cook this recipe for 2, 3, or 4 people. The only thing you have to do is convert the amount into double, triple, or quadruple. If the original recipe call for ½ cup of flour and you cooking for two. Then you will use 1cup of flour.**

Notes

SIDE-DISDES

- Stuffed Mushrooms w/ turkey bacon
- Lulu's Green Beans
- Roasted Brussels Sprouts
- Lemony Herbed Asparagus
- Mama's Macaroni & Cheese
- Butternut Squash with Carmel Onions
- Mama's Baked Beans
- Italian Stew Chickpeas
- Loaded Herbs Mashed Potatoes
- Healthy Coleslaw
- Mama's Potato Salad
- Mama's Macaroni Salad
- Lulu's Collar Beans
- Season Baked Kale Chips
- Hot Roasted Corn Salsa with shrimps
- Homemade Sausage
- Fluffy Scramble Eggs
- Mama's Red Rice
- Jamaican Style Peas and Rice
- Moroccan Craisins Squash Salad
- Mandarin Chickpeas Salad

Tips on food safety: **Rejecting Cans goods, when cans have swollen ends (indication of foodborne bacteria inside), leaks, rusted, dented, missing labels and out of dated. This also goes for packaged food.**

**Research Link:
http://ohioline.osu.edu/fresh/Storage.pd**

Notes

Stuff Mushrooms with Turkey Bacon

Ingredients:

5ea. Cremini mushrooms (clean and separated the stems)

2ea.Turkey bacon, (chopped)

1/4 tsp. Oregano, (dried)

1 Tbsp. Pimento, (can, or use red peppers chopped)

Pinch. Salt

Pinch. White Pepper

Pinch. Parsley, (dried)

1/4 tsp. Shallots, (minced)

1Tbsp. Parmesan cheese, (fresh grated)

1c. Fresh spinach, (chopped)

1tsp. Canola oil

Pam Spray

Preparation:

Heat the oven to 385 F.

Clean spinach and mushrooms thoroughly. In a sauté pan cook spinach and shallots in canola, until tender. In addition, most of the liquid from the spinach evaporated. Add pimento, oregano, salt, white pepper, and parsley; Mix well.

Place turkey bacon in oven until crispy. When done crumble turkey bacon and add it to the spinach mixture. Place mushrooms caps on a baking pan. Use a cookie sheet paper to cover the pan; then spray it with pam. Stuff the mushrooms mixture with a spoon. Bake in oven until mushrooms are tender. When done sprinkle Parmesan cheese on the top and bake for 5 minute or until cheese melted. Serve hot.

Tip: **This pairs very well with any main dish and any grated cheese**
Safety tip: **Use potholder when you take any pan out of the oven. It can prevent burns.**

Notes: **These recipes measured for one service, but you can convert any amount of service if you like. Example; if you want to cook this recipe for 2, 3, or 4 people. The only thing you have to do is convert the amount into double, triple, or quadruple. If the original recipe call for ½ cup of flour and you cooking for two. Then you will use 1cup of flour**

Lulu's Green Beans

Ingredients:

1Tbsp. Green beans (can)

1 Tbsp. Mushroom, (in slices)

1 Tbsp. Cabbage, (chopped small)

2ea. Bacon, (chopped small pieces)

1 tsp. Green peppers, (diced)

1 tsp. Red peppers, (diced)

1/2 c. Chicken stock

1/4 tsp. Onion powder

Pinch Salt

1/4 tsp. Black pepper

1/2 tsp. Shallot, (chopped)

Preparation:

In a frying pan, fry the bacon, after it is done set aside the bacon oil and the bacon pieces separately. Put the green beans into a bowl and add onion powder, salt, shallot, red peppers, green peppers, and black pepper; Mix well. Then take the cabbage, and mushrooms in and sauté them into a non-stick pan for 5 minutes. In a pot combine the green bean mixture, cabbage and mushrooms, bacon and the chicken stock, simmer for 10 minutes, and mix well. Serve hot.

Tips: You can use smoke turkey, lamb, chicken or salt pork.

Roasted Brussels sprouts

Ingredients:

1c. Brussels sprouts, (cut in halves)

1 tsp. Olive oil

1tsp. Onion, (finely chopped)

1tsp. Fresh thyme, (chopped)

1/2 tsp. Balsamic vinaigrette

1/2 tsp. Garlic powder

Pinch. Salt

Pinch. Black Pepper

Pam Spray

Preparations:

Preheat oven to 375F.

In a bowl, add Brussels sprouts, balsamic, garlic powder
and thyme and toss all together. Pour mixture onto a
greased, or pam spray baking sheet pan and put into
oven until golden brown. Then set aside in a saucepan,
add olive oil under medium heat. Add chopped onions
and cook until caramel; set aside. Sprinkle the caramel
onions on top of Brussels sprouts with salt and black
pepper. Serve hot.

Tip: This pairs very well with cacciatore sauce (Pg. 201) and slices of bruschetta.

Lemony Herbed Asparagus

Ingredients:

1 Tbsp. Olive oil

1 Tbsp. Butter, (non- salty)

1/4 tsp. Basil, (dried)

Pinch. Oregano, (dried)

1 tbsp. Lemon juice, (squeezed whole lemon)

Pinch. Black Pepper

Pinch. Salt

1/4 tsp. Thyme, (dried)

1 Cloves garlic, (minced)

1/4 Lb. Fresh asparagus spears, (trimmed, cut in three quarters)

Preparations:

Cut the asparagus bottom off and discard it, wash and dry with paper towel. In a sauté pan add asparagus, basil, oregano, thyme, garlic, salt and black pepper and sauté in olive oil until tender; stir frequently. Then remove from heat; set aside. In the same pan add butter and lemon juice and whisk together until it have a cloudy look. Transfer asparagus into lemon mixture and mix well. Serve hot

Tip: This pairs very well with chicken, pork, lamb, beef and liver.

Mama's Macaroni & Cheese

Ingredients:

1c. Macaroni

2 Tbsp. Olive oil

1/4 tsp. Salt

1Tbsp. White pepper

2c. water

1ea. Egg

3Tbsp. Milk, (can)

2 Tbsp. Butter, (melted)

2 Tbsp. Cheddar cheese, (extra sharp shredded)

2Tbsp. Mozzarella cheese, (shredded)

2Tbsp. Pepper jack cheese, (shredded)

2Tbsp. American cheese, (shredded)

2ea. Ramekin, (6oz or 9oz)

Preparation:

Preheat oven to 375 F.

Then you have to grease your ramekin and set aside. You can use a 6oz or 9oz ramekin to bake. Boil macaroni in salted water and olive oil until just tender or AL dente (Noodles will continue to bake in oven.). After noodles done, drain and set aside. Whisk egg in a large bowl, add milk, melted butter and stir in salt and white pepper except the cheeses. In a bowl combine noodles and cheeses; Mix well. Then pour in egg mixture and mix well. Pour into ramekin/s and set into oven until becomes bubbly and slight brown at edges an on top. Time to time take a knife and stick it into macaroni and cheese to see if it has done. When done remove from oven and let sit until it is cool down or serve hot.

Tip: **This pairs very well with collard greens, potatoes salad, and candy yam, corn bread.**

Butternut Squash with Carmel Onions

Ingredients:

1c. Butternut squash, (cut into cubes)

1 Tbsp. Butter, (melted)

1/4 tsp. Brown Sugar, (granulated)

1/4 c. Onions, (chopped)

1 tsp. Fresh parsley, (chopped)

 Pinch. Salt

Pinch. White pepper

Pinch. Thyme

¼ tsp. Fresh dill, (chopped)

Preparation:

In a sauté pan over low heat, melt butter, add onions, cook until caramel, and set aside. The butternut squash peel and remove the seeds. Add squash into pan and toss to coat with onions. Cook until squash is al dente and still holds it shape, stirring frequently. Then add sugar, thyme, dill, salt, and white pepper. Rewarm over medium heat before serving. When done sprinkle parsley on top and serve hot.

Mama's Baked Beans

Ingredients:

2ea. Slab salt fat (fat back)

2ea. slice bacon (fried, chopped)

4 oz. Kidney beans (best with can)

2ea. Cloves garlic (chopped)

1 Tbsp. Onion, (chopped)

1 Tbsp. Grape jelly

1 Tbsp. Ketchup

2 Tbsp. Worcestershire

1 Tbsp. Brown sugar

1 tsp. Black pepper

Pinch. Salt

1Tbsp. Syrup

1/4 tsp. Mustard

1/4 c. Orange juice

Pinch. Cinnamon

Preparation:

 In a frying pan, fry the salt pork on medium heat, when done take out the salt pork and set aside. Also, set aside the oil from the salt pork aside. In the same pan-fry the bacon also on medium heat and when it done; take out pan and set aside; same thing with the oil. Now in that same pan add kidney beans, salty fat, bacon, garlic, onion, jelly, ketchup, Worcestershire, brown sugar, black pepper, salt, syrup, mustard, orange juice, and cinnamon. Cook over low heat until evenly seasoning. Cook for 45 minutes to 1 hour. When done spoon it into a bowl and serve hot.

Notes: **These recipes measured for one service, but you can convert any amount of service if you like. Example; if you want to cook this recipe for 2, 3, or 4 people. The only thing you have to do is convert the amount into double, triple, or quadruple. If the original recipe call for ½ cup of flour and you cooking for two. Then you will use 1cup of flour**

Italian Stew Chickpeas

Ingredients:

1/2c. Chickpeas

1 Tbsp. Olive oil

1 Tbsp. Onions, (Finely diced)

2 tsp Garlic, (chopped)

1 tsp Poultry Seasoning

1/4 tsp Basil, (Dry, or ground)

2 Tbsp. Tomatoes Sauce

1/4 tsp. Fresh parsley, (finely chopped)

Pinch salt

1/4 tsp. Black pepper

Preparation:

In a pot combine onions, and garlic and heat over low heat with olive oil; cook until brown. Add poultry seasoning, black pepper, salt and basil and cook for a few minutes. Add tomatoes sauce, and blend well. Then add chickpeas, mix until incorporated. Turn heat up until it start to boil; then lower the heat down to a simmer and cook until the season are mix well. Set to cool down and serve hot; Garnish with chopped parsley.

Loaded Herbed Mashed Potatoes

Ingredients:

1 ea. Large potato, (boiled until soft)

2ea. Cloves garlic, (peeled and sliced)

2Tbsp. Cheddar cheese, (grated)

1/4 cup milk (or more)

1oz. Sour cream

1tsp. Basil, (chopped)

1tsp. Chives, (chopped)

1/4 tsp. fresh dill, (chopped)

1/4 tsp. Red onion, (chopped)

1/4 tsp. Green pepper

1/4 tsp. Red pepper

Pinch. Salt

Pinch. White pepper

Preparations:

In a pot of cold water add a pinch of salt and potato to boil for 25 minutes, or until the potato is very soft. Once soft take out of pot and set it in a ice bath or run cold water on it until it cool down. Peel and set aside. Heat the butter in a small saucepan. Add in the basil, garlic, chives, dill, red peppers, green peppers, red onions, salt and white pepper. Cook until vegetables are sweated and tender. Then set aside. Take the potato and mash it with the milk until creamy. "**Do not add vegetable mixture if you have lumps**". Continual to mash.Once creamy place on very low heat, stirring often. Cook until thick enough; add sour cream, and cheese. Stir until cheese melted. Pour vegetables in with the mash potatoes and stir well. Serve hot

Healthy Coleslaw

Ingredients:

1 c. Cabbages, (shredded)

1/4 tsp. Fresh parsley, (chopped)

1 tsp. Celery, (chopped)

1/4 tsp. Lemon juice

1oz. Sour cream, (creamy)

1 tsp. Sugar

1/4 tsp. Apple cider vinegar

1 Tbsp. Carrot, (shredded)

Pinch Salt

Pinch white pepper

Pinch. Fresh dill, (chopped)

Preparation:

In a bowl add shredded cabbages and carrot and mix well. Add parsley, celery, dill, lemon juice, sour cream, sugar, and apple cider vinegar and mix again well. Put in refrigerator overnight for ingredients can blend well. Before serving season it with salt and white pepper and serve cold.

Tip: **This recipe pairs well with any spicy food. It will calm your palate.**

Mama's Potato Salad

Ingredients:

1ea. Egg, (boiled)

1 tsp. Sweet relish, (drained)

1 Tbsp. Mayonnaise

2 ea. Medium potatoes, (diced)

1Tbsp. Onions, (chopped)

1/4tsp. Celery seed

1/2tsp. Red pepper, (chopped)

1/2tsp. Green pepper, (chopped)

Pinch. White pepper

1/4 tsp. Mustard

Pinch. Salt

Pinch. Fresh parsley, (chopped)

Pinch. Fresh dill, (chopped)

1c. Water

Preparations:

In a pot, add cold water, potatoes and egg to boil under medium heat. For the egg, spoon out after 3 minute. Run cold water over egg until egg cool down. Then diced egg and set aside. Continual cooking the potatoes until tender; drain well and wait until potatoes cool down. In a bowl add onions, salt, white pepper, celery seed, mustard, red pepper, green pepper; add potatoes, mayonnaise, eggs, sweet relish and mix well. Dust salad with parsley and dill. Sit in refrigerator about 2 hours and serve cold

Mama's Macaroni Salad

Ingredients:

3/4c. Uncooked macaroni

1ea. Egg, (boiled, diced)

2oz. Tuna, (can, drain)

1tsp. Onions, (finely chopped)

1/4 tsp. Green pepper, (chopped)

1/4 tsp. Red pepper, (chopped)

1/4 tsp. Celery, (finely diced)

1tsp. Sweet relish

1Tbsp.Mayonnaise

¼ tsp. Sour cream, (whipped)

Pinch. Parsley

Pinch. Onion powder

1/4 tsp. Mustard

Pinch. Salt

¼ tsp. White pepper

½ tsp. Paprika

1c. Water

1Tbsp. Olive oil

Preparations:

In pot of cold water, salt and ½ Tbsp. of olive oil cook macaroni until just tender, (al dente); drain in colander and rinse well under cold water; place macaroni in a bowl then add ½ Tbsp. of oil to prevent sticking and set aside. In the same bowl add in tuna, parsley, onion, red pepper, green peppers, celery and sweet relish and mix well; mayonnaise, sour cream, onion powder, mustard, white pepper, eggs; mix well. Sprinkle the top of the salad with paprika. Wrap with clear wrap and chill at least 1 hour before serving. Serve cold.

***Tip*: This pairs very well with saltine crackers.**

Lulu's Collar Beans

Ingredients:

1 bunch. Collard greens, (chopped, rinse well or frozen)

1ea. Smoked turkey wing, (cut into threes)

1/4 tsp. Garlic in oil, (jar)

½ Tbsp. Onion, (diced)

1/2 tsp. Red onion, (diced)

1/2 tsp. Celery, (chopped)

1/2 Tbsp. Apple cider vinegar

Pinch salt

1/4 tsp. Black pepper

3Tbsp. Pinto Beans, (can, wash and drain)

1 Tbsp. Canola oil

1c. Chicken stock

1c. Water, (or covered the turkey)

1/2 tsp. Sugar

1/4 tsp. Crush red pepper

Perpetration:

Place turkey wing into a pot of water to boil 1 hour or until tender. Then place collard greens with ½ Tbsp. oil, chicken stock, apple cider vinegar, salt, and black pepper; cover them and simmer until greens are tender.

Once tender, set aside for 1 hour. Then drain a little liquid out of the pot and set aside. Then in a sauté pan add ½ Tbsp. canola oil, onions, garlic, red onions, and celery until vegetables are firm. Do not drain. Add the vegetables, sugar, crush red pepper, and pinto beans to the greens: stir frequently. Test taste to see if it needs more salt. Uncover them every couple of minutes to look for consistency. If it have a little liquid and all the ingredients come together, it done. Serve hot.

Tip: **This pairs very well with hot sauce and corn bread.**

Notes: **These recipes measured for one service, but you can convert any amount of service if you like. Example; if you want to cook this recipe for 2, 3, or 4 people. The only thing you have to do is convert the amount into double, triple, or quadruple. If the original recipe call for ½ cup of flour and you cooking for two. Then you will use 1cup of flour**

Seasoned Baked Kale Chips

Ingredients:

1/2. Bunch kales, (rinsed and stems removed, cut into quarters)

1Tbsp. Hot Sauce, (optional)

1 Tbsp. Olive oil

1/4 tsp. Salt

1/4 tsp. Thyme, (dried)

Pinch. Rosemary, (dried)

1/4 tsp. Parsley, (dried)

Preparations:

Preheat oven to 375 F.

In a bowl mix kales, oil, thyme, rosemary, parsley and salt; toss it by hand. Try to cover all the leaves. Place on baking sheets separately and bake until they are crispy. After about 25 minutes, if it looks like they are not crispy. Place it back into oven and turn up the heat to 425°F. When done serve warm.

Tip: **This pairs very well with dipped melted chocolate. Grated cheese, or brown sugar.**

Note: **Time for baking varies depending on the size of your chips and desired crispness.**

Hot Roasted Pineapple Corn Salsa with Shrimps

Ingredients:

3 ea. Large shrimps, (clean and devein)

4oz. Sweet corn, (canned and drained)

1 ea. Roma tomatoes, (chopped)

1/2 tsp Red onions, (chopped)

½ Tbsp. Fresh cilantro, (minced)

1 tsp. Scotch bonnet, (chopped)

1tsp. Lime juice

1 Tbsp. Pineapples, (diced and roasted)

1 tsp. Green pepper, (Finely chopped)

1 tsp. Red pepper, (finely chopped)

1/2 tsp. Jalapeno pepper, (seeded, finely chopped)

Pinch. Salt

Pinch. White pepper, (optional)

16oz bg. Tortilla chips

1 pk. Rice cakes

Preparations:

Drain the can corn and place corn in a bowl; roast the pineapples and shrimps on grill just until done for 5 minutes on each side; take off grill and place aside. In a bowl add corn, shrimps, pineapple, tomatoes, red onions, and cilantro, scotch bonnet, lime juice, green peppers, red peppers, jalapeno, salt and white pepper and mix well. Set into refrigerator for 1 hour and serve cold or room temperature with tortilla chips or rice cakes.

Homemade Sausage

Ingredients:

Pinch. Sage, (dried)

1/4 tsp. Anis seeds

Pinch. Salt

1 tsp. Ground black pepper

Pinch. Marjoram, (dried)

1 tsp. Brown sugar

1/4 tsp. Crushed red pepper flakes

Pinch. Ground cloves

Pinch. Ground rosemary

3oz. Ground pork

Preparations:

In a bowl combine all ingredients, combine the sage, salt, ground black pepper, marjoram, brown sugar, and crushed red pepper and ground cloves, rosemary and mix well. Then place the pork in non-stick frying pan until golden brown. Serve hot.

Tip: This pairs very well with eggs, grits, and toasted bun

Fluffy Scramble Eggs

Ingredients:

2 tsp Butter, (cold)

1ea. Eggs

1tsp. Milk, (low fat milk)

Pinch. Salt

Pinch. Black pepper

Pam Spray (optional)

Preparation:

In a bowl whisk the eggs, 1tsp. butter, and milk until the eggs mixture is all yellow; add salt and black pepper until it well combined. Heat the other 1tsp. butter in a sauté pan over medium –low heat, or used a nonstick pan and spray it with pam. Pour eggs into the pan, stir constantly until it have reached desired consistency. Placed the eggs into plate and serve hot.

Tip: you can add cheese, vegetables, bacon, sausages, or anything you like but this recipe pairs very well with wheat toast....Testing your eggs. If it floats, throw it away. Get a glass of water and gently place an egg into the glass of water, and if it sink to the bottom, the egg is good but if it float to the top it is not good.

Mama's Red Rice

Ingredients:

1/2 c. Rice, (uncooked parboiled)

1 ea. Slice bacon, (chopped, fry it and set aside)

1 Tbsp. Onion, (chopped)

1 Tbsp. Red peppers, (chopped)

1 Tbsp. Green peppers, (chopped)

1 tsp. Tomatoes paste, (canned) 1

Tbsp. Tomato sauce, (canned)

1 c. Water

1/4 tsp. Ground chili powder

Pinch. Salt

1/4 tsp. Black pepper

Preparations:

In a pot, fry the bacon on low heat. When it done, take out the bacon, set aside. Then leave the bacon oil in the pot; add green peppers, red peppers, rice and onions; simmer over medium-heat until vegetables are tender. Then you add the tomatoes paste, bacon (chopped) and tomato sauce. Stir until everything is well blended. Add water chili powder, black pepper and salt and lower the heat and cover with a paper tower, and lid; stir frequently. Cook until all liquid is absorbed and rice is fluffy. Remove from heat and allow to sit. Take a fork to fluff and serve hot.

Tip: This recipe pairs very well with just about any main dishes. In addition, you can use chicken stock to replace the water, kidney beans, sofrito, adobo, ground achiote, olives, or ham (diced), and you have Spanish rice. In addition, if you add jalapeno with all the extra ingredients you have Mexican rice.

Jamaican Style Peas and Rice

Ingredients:

1/4 c. Red kidney (or black beans)

1ea. Scallion, (whole)

10ea. Permento, (whole allspice)

1/4 tsp Thyme (dry)

1/2 c. Parboil rice, (uncooked)

1/4 tsp. Salt

1/4 c. Coconut (or coconut milk from can)

1/2 tsp. Olive oil

1c. Water

Preparation:

Coconut- open coconut and drain the coconut juice; set aside. Now scoop out coconut and dice it; put diced coconut in a food processor and finely grated; place coconut into a cheesecloth and squeeze the juice into a cup and set aside.

In a pot you put in 1c. Water. Then you add your beans, coconut milk, scallions, thyme, salt, and permento and cook on low heat until it comes to a boil. Then you add your rice and olive oil. Stir rice until all the ingredients is mix well. Cook on a low heat and cover the top of the pot with paper towel, then put lid on top and cook until done.

Tip: You can use the excess coconut from the cheesecloth to make homemade ices and/or throw it away. Take the coconut juice from the coconut and excess coconut; mix well and place it in an ice tray with a toothpick center. Wait until it freezes and eat...Also you can add chopped scotch bonnet into the rice if you like heat in your food.

Notes: These recipes measured for one service, but you can convert any amount of service if you like. Example; if you want to cook this recipe for 2, 3, or 4 people. The only thing you have to do is convert the amount into double, triple, or quadruple. If the original recipe call for ½ cup of flour and you cooking for two. Then you will use 1cup of flour.

Moroccan Craisins Squash Salad

Ingredients:

2 c. Squash, (cube)

1 Tbsp. Craisins

1 Tbsp. Cucumbers, (diced)

½ tsp. Cilantro, (chopped)

1/8 tsp. Scallion

1/8 tsp. Red onions

1 Tbsp. Green beans

1 /2. Apple, (slices, red delicious)

Dressing:

1 tsp. Lemon juice, (fresh juice from lemons)

¼ c. Oil, (Olive)

1/8 tsp. Garlic, (garlic in oil)

Pinch. Salt

1/8 tsp. White pepper

½ tsp. Cumin

Pinch. Cinnamon

1/8 tsp. Cayenne pepper

1 tsp. Honey

2 Tbsp. Chipotle ranch dressing

Preparations:

In a pot of water, add a pinch of salt and a dash of oil. Add the squash and cook for 10 minutes or until tender. After the squash is done set it into an ice bath to stop the process of cooking. Once the squash has cool down. Set in the refrigerator for 1 hour. Take out the refrigerator and in a bowl add apples, green beans, red onions, cilantro, cucumbers, and raisins. Toss to mix well.

In another bowl, add lemon juice, oil, garlic, salt, white pepper, cumin, cinnamon, cayenne pepper, honey, and chipotle dressing. Whisk it together well. Pour dressing over salad serve cold.

Mandarin Chickpeas Salad

Ingredients:

2 ea. Mandarin, (peeled and section)

1 c. Chickpeas, (canned, wash

1 Tbsp. Green pepper, (diced)

1 Tbsp. Red pepper, (diced) 1

tsp. Red onion, (chopped) 1

Tbsp. Roma tomatoes, (diced)

Dressing:

1 Tbsp. Orange juice

2 Tbsp. Honey

Pinch. Salt

Pinch. White pepper

1 Tbsp. Apple cider vinegar

Preparations:

Peel the mandarin and section them. Place in a bowl. In the bowl, add tomatoes, green peppers, red peppers, red onions, and chickpeas. Toss and mix well. For the dressing, in another bowl add orange juice, honey, salt, white pepper, and apple cider vinegar. Whisk all ingredients together until well blended. Pour dressing gently over the mandarin salad, and mix well. Use as much as need and save the rest for later. Set in refrigerator to serve cold.

Main Dishes

- Mangu Dish
- Grits with Cheese
- Waffle with Egg Benedict
- Kale Egg Omelet
- Homemade Blueberry Pancakes
- Belgian Waffles with Mushroom & Spinach topping
- Mama's Smoke Neck Bone & Black eye peas
- Mama's Six Seasoning Fish (Whiting)
- Smothered pork chop with onions and broccoli
- Sockeye Salmon with Quinoa Salad
- Curry Seafood Rice
- Curry Goat
- Spicy Romary Chicken
- Stew Pig feet with Kidney Beans and Black Beans
- Chicken & Dumping
- Spaghetti & Shrimps with Clam Sauce
- Seasoned Vegetables Skewers
- Lemon Braised lamb
- Jive Turkey with Cranberry Sauce
- Pad Thai
- Mama's Cabbage with Turkey Meatballs
- Stuffed Peppers with Chicken
- Ratatouille
- Mama's Southern Gumbo

Notes

Mangu Dish

Ingredients:

1ea. Egg (fried sunny side up)

1ea. Plantains, (unripe, cut into pieces)

3 sl. Salami, (Higueral, slices)

2 sl. Queso Frito, (fried cheese)

1/2 Tbsp. Butter

1/2. Red onions, (slices into rings)

1/2 tsp. Canola oil

1/4 tsp. Vinegar

1/4c. Cold water

1/4 tsp. Salt

½ tsp. Black pepper

Pinch. Onion powder

Preparations:

In a pot of cold water, add salt and place on medium heat. Place the plantains and cook until the plantains are tender about 15-20 minutes. Take pot off the heat and set aside. In a sauté pan, add canola oil, black pepper and sauté onions; when onions are soft set aside. In a non-stick pan, fry salami and cheese, then scramble the eggs. However, after every use wipe pan out.

Take the plantains out of the water and proceed to mash them with a fork or mash potato masher. Add the butter and a little water and keep mashing until the consistency is very smooth. Plate the plantains with red onions on top, cheese, salami and eggs and serve hot.

Tip: This pairs very well with Morir Sonando (milk, sugar, ice and orange juice)

Notes: These recipes measured for one service, but you can convert any amount of service if you like. Example; if you want to cook this recipe for 2, 3, or 4 people. The only thing you have to do is convert the amount into double, triple, or quadruple. If the original recipe call for ½ cup of flour and you cooking for two. Then you will use 1cup of flour.

Grits with Cheese

Ingredients:

1c. Water

1/2 tsp. butter

2 ½ Tbsp. Uncooked quick-cooking grits

1/4 tsp. Salt

1 oz. Cream cheese

1 tsp. Ground white pepper

Preparations:

Bring water to a boil in a small pot. Slowly stir in grits and salt. Cover and reduce heat very low, stirring occasionally until mixture thickened. Add cream cheese and stirring until cheese has melted. After grits is done, placed into a bowl add butter and sprinkle black pepper on top of grits. Serve hot

Tips: **You can use Cheddar Cheese, shredded extra-sharp Cheddar cheese, Parmesan cheese, or American cheese. You also can put the grits in the oven on 350 degrees with cheese sprinkle on top.**

Safety Notices: **WARNING! Make sure that the pot of grits are cover with a lid. Because when the grits are cooking it can pop out of the pot. In addition, you can get burn. When done remove from heat before taking off the lid.**

Waffle with Egg Benedict

Ingredients:

2ea. Eggs

1 c. Water

1/4c. Vinegar

2 Tbsp. Hollandaise, (pg. 212)

Pinch. Salt

Pinch. White pepper

2ea. Waffles, (store bought, wheat)

6ea. Cherry tomatoes, (sliced in halves)

1pk .Spinach, (frozen)

Preparations:

In a sauté pan place the spinach over medium heat and covered until spinach is unfrozen. Take the lid off and continual to cook until all liquid evaporate and spinach is soft. Add salt and white pepper. Continual cooking for 5 minute. Then set aside. Set waffle into toaster oven to toast on both sides.

Place water and vinegar in a small pot on high heat until boiling. Gently break eggs into a bowl, easily place into water. Cook for 2 minutes or (more if needed). Let eggs stand, until the eggs turn all white. With a slotted spoon, remove eggs from water; place on top of the waffles, then add slices of cherry tomatoes, spinach and Spoon some hollandaise sauce over each waffle. Sever hot

Kale Egg Omelet

Ingredients:

½ Small onion, (minced)

1/2 Tsp. Cloves garlic, (minced)

1/4 c. Kale, (remove stems and chopped)

2ea. Eggs, (or eggs white)

1 Tbsp. Shredded mozzarella cheese

Pinch. Salt

Pinch. White pepper

Preparations:

In a sauté pan, sauté the onion over low heat stirring frequently. Add garlic and kales and cook until kales are soft. In a bowl beat eggs, add salt and white pepper. Fry egg omelet style, after eggs omelet done. Pour evenly over kale mixture. Cover and cook on low heat until hot enough; Sprinkle the mozzarella cheese. In addition, allow cheese to melt. Cut in half and serve hot.

Homemade Blueberry Pancakes

Ingredients:

2 Tbsp. Milk, (low-fat)

1/2c. All-purpose flour

 Pinch. Lemon, (grated zest)

¼ tsp. Vanilla

1ea. Egg

 2 Tbsp. Sugar

1tsp. Salt

1tsp. Baking soda

2Tbsp. Butter

2/3c. Blueberries, (fresh and wash)

¼ tsp. Maple syrup

Preparation:

In a mixing bowl combine the milk, flour, vanilla, sugar, salt and baking soda; beat the egg and add to flour mixture. Mix until everything is blend thoroughly; stir in melted butter. Rest dough for 20 minutes. In a sauté pan add blueberries cook on low heat for 5 minutes; Place pancake mixture over medium heat on a preheated griddle or sauté pan until bubbles appear or until golden brown. Turn pancake, continue until cook through, and browned on both sides. Serve while warm with a drizzle of maple syrup.

Tip: This pairs very well with homemade sausages. You also can use sugar substitute in recipe.

Belgian Waffles with Mushroom & Spinach Topping

Ingredients:

2oz.Chopped spinach, (frozen)

1oz.Mushrooms, (sliced)

1ea. Egg

2Tbsp. Parmesan cheese, (grated)

Pinch. Salt

Pinch Black pepper

1/4 tsp. Ground garlic

2 ea. Belgian waffles, (store brought)

Preparations:

Defrost spinach overnight. Next day cook spinach into a sauté pan until unfrozen and soft; squeeze out excess liquid. Add mushrooms salt, black pepper, and garlic. Cook 10 minutes; mix in eggs until eggs done and set aside. Place waffles into toaster until both sides are brown. Plate the waffles and pour spinach mixture over them, then sprinkle grated cheese over spinach mixture. Serve hot.

Mama's Smoke Neck Bone & Black eye peas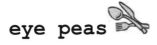

Ingredients:

1/4c. Black-eyed peas, (dried, soak overnight)

1c. Chicken broth, (low-sodium)

2oz. Smoked ham hock

2oz. Smoke neck bone

1Tbsp.Onion, (chopped)

1Tbsp. Celery, (chopped)

1 Tbsp. Carrots, (diced)

1 Tsp. Jalapeno pepper, (seeded, minced, and optional)

1 tsp. Thyme, (dried)

Preparations:

In a pot of water, boil ham-hock for 2 hours over medium heat. After 1 hour pour the salty water out and renew more water into the pot, repeat every 30 minutes until the salty taste is gone. Second hour check to see if the ham-hock should be tender. If not, continual to cook until ham hock is tender; Place black-eyed peas and smoke neck bones; cover pot, and if you need more water, add more not too deep over peas and meat. In addition, continual to a boil until peas and meat is tender. Add onions, celery, carrots, and jalapenos (optional), to the black-eyed peas and meat; bring to a boil. Reduce heat and cook, covered, for about 1 hour, or until vegetables are tender, stirring occasionally. When all done serve, hot.

Safety notes: WARNING! The scotch bonnets is very hot. Make sure to wear gloves and DO NOT rub your eyes with the gloves.

Notes: These recipes measured for one service, but you can convert any amount of service if you like. Example; if you want to cook this recipe for 2, 3, or 4 people. The only thing you have to do is convert the amount into double, triple, or quadruple. If the original recipe call for ½ cup of flour and you cooking for two. Then you will use 1cup of flour

Mama's Six Seasoning Fish
(Whiting)

Ingredients:

2ea. Whiting fish, (deboned, wash and filet)

½c. Flour, (all-purpose)

1 Tbsp. Cornmeal

¼ tsp. Salt

1 tsp. Black pepper

1 tsp. Old Bay Seasoning

1c. canola oil, (for frying)

1 tsp. Garlic Powder

Pinch. Ground paprika

Pinch. Ground curry powder

Pinch. Ground cayenne pepper

Preparations:

Lay fish on plate; season fish with salt, black pepper, old bay, garlic powder, paprika, curry, cayenne pepper. Season on both sides. In a bowl or brown paper bag, or plastic bag. Add flour and cornmeal and shake the bag until the fish is cover with the flour mixture Pre- heat frying pan on stove with canola oil. Shake the fish excess flour off the fish into the bag before putting it into the oil. Brown on both sides and place fish on paper towels to drain. Serve hot with a sprinkling of malt vinegar.

Tips: Canola Oil- good to use in many foods such as meat marinades, casseroles, salad dressings and baked goods. Olive Oil- take advantage of these benefits, substitute olive oil for saturated fats such as butter and shortening in cooking. Store olive oil in a cool, dark place, as it is sensitive to light and heat.

Smothered pork chop with onions, and broccoli

Ingredients:

1ea. Pork chop, (wash and clean)

1 Tbsp. Flour, (all-purpose)

1 tsp. Cornstarch

Pinch. Garlic powder

1 Tbsp. Green pepper, (julienne)

1 Tbsp. Red pepper, (julienne)

3oz. Broccoli, (chopped stems off)

Pinch. Black pepper

1/4 tsp. Salt

1c. Water

1/2 Onions, (sliced)

1/4c. Canola oil

Pam Spray

Preparations:

Clean and place pork chop on plate and season with salt, black pepper, and garlic; set aside for about 1 hour. Place pork chop into frying pan with oil and sear it on both side for 5 minutes; remove to paper towels, set aside. In the same frying pan; add onions, green peppers, and red peppers until tender; add flour and stir until flour is brown. Place the pork chop into pan with the onions mixture; add water and cover pork chop and cook on low heat. Stir in cornstarch mixture (combine cornstarch and cold water until cornstarch resolve in cup). Cook until it become thickens, stirring constantly; adjust as needed while pork chop is still cooking. Steam broccoli for 5minutes or until the broccoli soften. Plate pork chop, set broccoli on side, and pour gravy over broccoli. Serve hot

Tip: This pairs very well with brown rice.

Sockeye Salmon with Quinoa Salad

Quinoa Salad

Ingredients:

1c. Quinoa

1/2 Tbsp. Canola oil

2c. Water

Pinch. Oregano, (dried)

Pinch. Thyme, (dried)

1 Tbsp. Green Pepper, (chopped)

1 Tbsp. Red pepper, (chopped)

1 tsp. Fresh parsley, (chopped)

1 tsp. Apple cider vinegar

Pinch. Salt

1/4 tsp. Fresh lemon, (grated rinds)

Pinch. Black pepper

Preparations:

In a pot of cold water, place the quinoa. Cook over low medium heat and cook until quinoa makes cracking and popping noises/tender. In a saucepan add canola oil; stir thyme, oregano, green peppers, red peppers, parsley, salt, apple cider vinegar, lemon rind, and black pepper. Simmer; covered until quinoa done. Fluff with a fork and set in refrigerator about 1 hour. Serve cold.

Sock eye Salmon

Ingredients:

Pinch. White pepper

Pinch. Salt

1/4 tsp. Fresh dill

Pinch. Ground garlic powder

4oz. Salmon fillets

1ea. Chicken bouillon

1 tsp. Canola oil

1/4.tsp. Soy sauce

1Tbsp. Scallions, (finely chopped)

4 sl Lemon, (thinly sliced)

2 slices onions, (rings)

Preparations:

In a saucepan; place canola oil over medium heat; Place salmon, white pepper, salt, and garlic powder and sear for 3 minutes on each side; set aside. In a pot, add chicken bouillon, soy sauce, onions and scallions. Cook until vegetables are tender. Pour vegetables over salmon and cook together for 5 minutes. Set aside for ½ hour; cover and chill for 1 hour. Drain and discard marinade. Plate the salmon, and then place lemon rings and vegetables mixture on top. Serve cold

Curry Seafood Rice

Ingredients:

1c. Parboil rice

1Tbsp. Onion

1 Tbsp. Red pepper, (chopped)

1 Tbsp. Green pepper, (chopped)

1tsp. Carrot, (grated)

1tsp. Celery, (chopped)

1/2 Scallions, (chopped)

1oz. cod fish, (The cod fish must be cooked until unsalted)

1oz. Shrimp, (clean and devein)

1oz. Crabmeat, (shredded)

1/4. Clam juice, (store brought)

1/4 tsp. Red wine, (store brought)

1tsp.Ground garlic powder

1 Tbsp. Ground curry powder

Pinch. Salt

1/4 tsp. Black pepper

1tsp. Thyme

1c. Water

2 Tbsp. Canola oil

Preparations:

In a pot add cold water and rice; Add onion, red peppers, green peppers, curry powder, red wine, carrot, celery, scallion, garlic powder, salt, thyme, black pepper, and canola oil. Stir all ingredients together and stir consistency over high heat until rice comes to a boil. Add all the seafood, mix rice well, cover top with paper towel, put lid on top, stirring frequently over a low heat until a fork, and fluff the rice. Serve hot

Curry Goat

Ingredients:

1/2 lbs. Goat meat

½ Onions, (chopped)

2 Tbsp. Ground curry powder

½ Tbsp. thyme, (dried)

1 tsp. Ground cayenne pepper

Pinch. Black pepper (if needed)

1/4 tsp. Salt

2 Tbsp. Canola oil

Preparation:

Place meat in plastic bag with curry powder, thyme, black pepper and salt; refrigerate overnight. Next day cook meat in large saucepan with water over low-heat. Add oil and simmer about 2 hour or until the meat is tender and brown. Add onion, and cayenne pepper. Simmer 15 more minutes. Best serve hot with pea and rice.

Tip: This pairs very well with Jamaican style peas and rice receipt on pg.121

Spicy Rosemary Chicken

Ingredients:

3oz. Chicken breast (wash and pat dry)

1ea. Clove garlic, (finely chopped)

1 Tbsp. Butter

½ small green pepper, (cut Julianne)

1 sm. Onion (cut thick rings)

½ small red pepper, (cut Julianne)

⅓ tsp. Apple cider vinegar

Pinch. Fresh dill, (chopped)

1/2 tsp. Rosemary, (dried, use extra if needed)

1/4 tsp. Cayenne pepper

Pinch. Salt

Pinch. White pepper

1Tbsp. Italian dressing

Preparations:

Wash and clean chicken. In a saucepan add butter, cayenne pepper and place chicken; cook chicken on both sides until golden brown, about 5 min each side. Then add garlic, onions, rosemary, Italian dressing, green pepper, red pepper, salt, and white pepper; cook about 2 minutes until vegetables are soft, sprinkle some dill on top. Serve hot

Tip: This recipe pairs very well with extra rosemary sprinkle on top and grated parmesan cheese. For extra spicy, add chopped scotch bonnet. In addition, it will bring some fire to your palate.

Stew Pig feet with Kidney beans and Black beans

Ingredients:

1ea. Pig feet, (wash, cut into three)

1/2 Onion, (chopped)

1/2c. White vinegar

2oz. Pigs tails (wash, cut into pieces)

1oz. Pig ears, (wash, cut into pieces)

1 Tbsp. Fresh celery, (chopped)

1 Tbsp. Green pepper, (chopped)

1 Tbsp. Red pepper, (chopped)

¼ c. Black beans (dry and rinsed)

¼ c. Kidney beans (dry and rinsed)

1ea.Chicken bouillon, (cubes)

1/4 tsp. Ground garlic powder

Pinch. Ground onion power

1/4 tsp. red crush pepper

1/4 tsp. Worcestershire sauce

1/4 tsp. Salt

1/2 tsp. Black pepper

1Tbsp. Hot sauce

1/2 tsp. Adobo seasoning

Water, (pour until water covered the pork)

Preparations:

In a soup pot of cold water and vinegar; add washed pig feet, ears, and tails and pour water until it's covered.(use knife to remove hairs from pig feet).Boil pig feet mixture for 1 hour. Set all vegetables aside. After 1 hour, pour out water, rinse pigs feet mixture. Rinse out pot, put pigs mixture back into the pot, cover it with more water and boil it again. Place adobo, black pepper, salt, Worcestershire sauce, red crush pepper, onion powder, garlic powder, onions, green peppers, red peppers, chicken bouillon, and celery, kidney beans and black beans. Bring to a boil on medium heat, cover and occasionally stir until beans and pig mixture are soft. If water evaporates, pour more water into pot. Serve hot

Tip: **Serve over a bed of white rice; also add hot sauce for a greater taste.**

Notes: **These recipes measured for one service, but you can convert any amount of service if you like. Example; if you want to cook this recipe for 2, 3, or 4 people. The only thing you have to do is convert the amount into double, triple, or quadruple. If the original recipe call for ½ cup of flour and you cooking for two. Then you will use 1cup of flour**

Chicken & Dumping

Ingredients

3oz. Chicken beast, (cut up into cube)

1ea. Bouquet garni, (recipe follows)

Salt, (as needed)

1c. Sweet peas and carrots, (can brought)

Roux, (pg. 208)

1c.Water, (more if needed)

1tsp. Onion, (chopped)

1/4 tsp. Adobo

Dumplings

5 Tbsp. All-purpose flour

1/3 c. Water

Pinch. Salt

Pinch. Thyme

Bouquet Garni

1ea. Bay leaf

3ea. Peppercorns

1 ea. Stalk of celery (cut double thick)

1/4 tsp. Margarine

1 ea. Cheesecloth, (add bay leaf, peppercorns, celery, and margarine in middle of cheesecloth and tie tight.)

Preparations:

In a pot over medium heat, add water, chicken, onions, adobo and bouquet garni to boil. Then add salt; cook until chicken is tender. Add roux to thicken the chicken liquid; if liquid evaporate add more water. Set chicken aside.

Dumplings: In a large bowl, sift flour, salt, and thyme. Add water slowly until it mixed to a form dough. After the dough is thicken, use your fingers to pinch off some dough and drop dumplings into chicken mixture. Cover and simmer until dumplings done. Continual cooking slowly until all ingredients mixed. Serve hot in a bowl.

Tip: **This recipe go very well with egg noodles.**

Spaghetti & Shrimps with Clam Sauce

Ingredients:

3oz. Shrimps (deveined and wash)

1/2lb. Spaghetti

1 Tbsp. Butter

Pinch. Salt

Pinch. White pepper

1ea. Cloves garlic, (finely chopped)

1 Tbsp. Onion, (finely chopped)

2ea Cherry clams, (saved drained liquid, and chopped)

½ Pot water

1 Tbsp. Canola oil

¼ tsp. Ground thyme

1/2/ tsp. Parsley

1Tbsp. Green pepper, (chopped)

1 Tbsp. Red pepper, (chopped)

Preparations:

In a pot of water over high heat, add salt, and canola oil. Wait for water to boil; add spaghetti and stir with a fork constantly until spaghetti is al dente (firm but not tender); rinse off spaghetti in a colander with cold water, then set aside.

In a saucepan over medium heat, place butter, garlic, onions, celery, green pepper, red pepper, thyme, clams, white pepper and shrimps. Braise until tender but not brown; add the spaghetti and drain clams, reserving juice and mix well. Turn heat down on low heat. Place into a bowl and sprinkle parsley on top and serve hot.

Tip: this recipe pairs very well topped with Parmesan cheese on top.

Seasoned Vegetables Skewers

Ingredients:

2oz. Chicken breast, (cut into cubes)

2ea. Skewers

1/2ea. Yellow Onions, (cut into wedges)

1/2ea. Green squash, (cut in halves)

1/2ea. Green pepper (cut in wedges)

1/2ea. Red pepper (cut in wedges)

Pinch. Parsley

1ea. Polish sausage (cut in sectional)

1/2lb. Shrimps, (raw, deveined)

1/2c. Whole mushrooms

1/4 tsp. Adobo

Preparations:

Preheat grill around about ½ hour; Place onions, chicken, squash, shrimp, green peppers, polish sausage, red peppers, and mushrooms onto skewer; sprinkle with adobo seasoning. Then grill until shrimps and sausages done; garnish with parsley. Serve warm.

Lemon Braised lamb

Ingredients:

3oz. Lamb chop (wash and dry)

1/2ea. Onion, (sliced)

1/2 tsp. Olive oil

4 sl. Lemon, (thinly sliced)

4sl. Orange, (thinly sliced)

1/2pk. Beef stock

2Tbsp. Red wine

1/4 tsp. Honey

Pinch. Salt

Pinch. Ground black pepper

1/4 tsp. Thyme

Preparations:

In a sauté pan, add oil and heat oven low heat until oil is almost smoking. Add the lamb chop and brown on both sides about 5 minutes. If it not brown on both side in 5 minutes, flip it and cook it for another 5 minutes. After it's done add in the onion and adjust the heat down to medium; cook until the onion is wilted and pale; add in the lemon and orange slices, stock, red wine, honey, salt, thyme and black pepper. Bring the liquid to a boil;

stir to combine all the ingredients together. Cover and simmer until the lamb chop is very tender take off heat and Serve hot.

Tip: **This recipe pairs very well with cooked pasta or bulgur.**

Jive Turkey with Cranberry Sauce

Ingredients:

3oz of sliced Turkey, (turkey breast or process sliced turkey)

1Tbsp. Orange juice

1 Tbsp. Dry white wine

1/2c. Fruit cocktail, (fruit juice only)

¼ tsp. cranberries, (dried)

1 Tbsp. Water

1/4 tsp. Onion, (minced)

Pinch. Salt

Preparations:

In a sauté pan, add water, salt, cranberries, wine, orange juice, cocktail juice, and onions; cover and cook over low heat until cranberries are plump; Stir consistently. Add turkey and simmer until meat is no longer pink. If liquid have evaporate, add more water for thickness. Serve hot.

Tip: This recipe pairs very well serve over loaded mash potatoes and holla greens

Pad Thai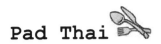

Ingredients:

4ea.Large shrimps, (devein)

1oz. Crab meat, (chopped)

1oz. Pad Thai rice noodles

1 tsp. Tofu, (bean curd, cubes)

1ea. Small egg

1/2 tsp. Canola oil

1/2 Tbsp. Bean sprout

Pinch. Thai fish sauce

1/4 tsp. Syrup

1ea. Clove garlic, (chopped)

1/8 tsp. Scotch bonnet

1/4 tsp. Chives, (chopped)

1/2 Tbsp. Thai sweet chilies, (sauce store brought)

1ea. Lime, (slices)

Preparation

Place Pad Thai rice noodles in a bowl; pour some hot water and cover it, Soak until tender; drain and set aside. In a sauté, pan heat oil and add vegetable over medium heat until medium done. Add egg, crabmeat and shrimp. Stir until shrimp, crabmeat and egg are almost cooked. Add tofu and Thai sweet chilies; cook for 20 seconds; add Pad Thai rice noodles and cook for 2 minute. Stir in bean sprouts, Thai fish sauce, scotch bonnet, and syrup and cook until noodles absorb sauce and noodles well coated. Stir in garlic then transfer to serving plates. Serve hot or cold.

Tip: Sprinkle with slices limes and chives to garnish.

Safety Tips: WARNING! The scotch bonnets is very hot. Make sure to wear gloves and DO NOT rub your eyes with the gloves.

Safety food Tips: When purchasing fish frozen or fresh PLEASE check for signs of spoilage, concave eyes, grayness, body to soft, brown pupil, opaque, discolored red cornea, brown gills, and flakes. In addition, storing fresh fish are a piece of work. Frozen fish can Stored Up to 9 Mos. Fresh fish best consumed 1-2 days of purchase. Store In the coldest portion of the refrigerator 40°F.

My Sister (Desiree Williams Henderson) and I

Mama's Cabbage with Turkey Meatballs

Ingredient

1/4c. Chicken bouillon

1 Tbsp. Smoked kielbasa, (cut into small pieces)

1tsp. Onion, (chopped)

1 tsp. Butter

1 tsp. Green pepper, (chopped)

1 tsp. Red pepper, (chopped)

1/2 Cabbage, (small size, julienne)

Pinch. Salt

Pinch. Ground cayenne pepper, (optional)

Pinch. Black pepper

Pinch. Sage

1/2c.Ground Turkey

Preparations

Place ground turkey in a bowl, add black pepper, salt and sage, mix well. Use your hand and round out turkey into meatball. In a sauté pan add butter and meatballs; Cover and cook until golden brown over medium –low heat. When done take them out of the pan and set aside.

Wash pan.

In that same sauté pan, brown sausage over medium heat. Add onion, green pepper, red pepper and cook until vegetables are a little brown; Remove from heat and set aside. In a pot, add cabbage, chicken bouillon and cook until cabbage is tender, stirring occasionally. Uncover and add turkey meatballs, sausages, and peppers mixture. Mix (if liquid evaporate, add a little water). Seasoned with the cayenne pepper, (optional) and cook 5 minutes more. Serve hot

Tip: This recipe pairs very well with, over rice or as a side dish with some cornbread. You also can use ground beef or ground chicken.

Stuffed Peppers with Chicken

Ingredients

3oz. Ground chicken

1ea. Green pepper (cut in half, long)

1/4c. Rice, (cooked)

1c. Water

1Tbsp. Canola oil

1/8 tsp. Basil

1/8 tsp. Oregano

1/4 tsp. Garlic, (fresh, chopped)

1/4c. Tomato sauce

1Tbsp. Bread crumbs

1/8. Black pepper

Pinch. Salt

1 tsp. Onion, (finely chopped)

Preparations

Preheat oven to 375°F.

In a pot, add water, oil, salt and rice. Cook rice under medium heat until rice come to a boil; lower heat and cover until rice is fluffy. When done set aside. In a colander, rinse the green halves pepper well under cold water to remove any seeds and set aside. Place ground chicken into sauté pan. Cook until chicken is almost brown; add onions, black pepper, basil, and oregano, stir occasionally until all ingredients mixed well. Add breadcrumbs and toss mixture. Grease a sheet pan; stuff the halves pepper with the chicken mixture, sprinkle with a little more breadcrumbs, and place it in the baking pan. Bake until golden brown. Remove from the oven and pour juices over pepper from the pan. Serve hot.

Ratatouille

Ingredients:

1 Tbsp. Olive oil

½ tsp. Black beans, (canned, wash and drained)

1 Tbsp. Eggplant, (cubed)

1 tsp. Winter squash, (diced)

1 tsp. Sweet corn, (canned, or ear of corn boiled and shave off)

1 Tbsp. Zucchini, (cubed)

Pinch. Salt

Pinch. Black pepper

Pinch. Cayenne pepper

1 tsp. Onion, (chopped)

1Tbsp. Celery, (diced)

1tsp. Green pepper, (dice)

1tsp. Red pepper, (dice)

1 ea. Fresh basil leaves

2 tsp. Apple cider vinegar

1 Tbsp. Tomato, (diced in sauce)

Pinch. Red pepper flakes

1ea. Cloves garlic, (minced)

Pinch curry powder

1/2 tsp. Oregano, (dried)

Pinch Thyme, (fresh)

Preparations:

Preheat oil in a large skillet over medium-low heat; add eggplant, squash, zucchini, onion, corn, celery, green pepper, black beans, and red pepper, cook 2 minutes. Add cider vinegar, diced tomato, garlic, curry powder, salt, black pepper, cayenne pepper, red pepper flakes, basil, thyme and oregano; simmer until liquid is slightly reduced heat to low and continual cooking until all ingredients are mixed well. Transfer mixture in to pot, add a 1/2 c. of water, and simmer about 5-10 minutes. Serve hot

Notes: These recipes measured for one service, but you can convert any amount of service if you like. Example; if you want to cook this recipe for 2, 3, or 4 people. The only thing you have to do is convert the amount into double, triple, or quadruple. If the original recipe call for ½ cup of flour and you cooking for two. Then you will use 1cup of flour.

Mama's Southern Gumbo

Ingredients:

1 Tbsp. Oil

1/8 tsp. Onions, (Diced)

¼ tsp. Green pepper, (diced)

1/4c. Garbanzo Beans, (canned drained)

4 ea. Shrimps, (clean and devein)

4oz. White potato, (canned)

1Tbsp. Tomatoes sauce

Pinch. Onion powder

1 Tbsp. Cut okra

1/4 tsp. Ground paprika

Pinch. Ground cinnamon

Pinch. Ground ginger powder

Pinch. Ground cumin

1/8 tsp. Thyme, (dried)

1/8 tsp. Salt

1/8 tsp. Black Pepper

1c.Water

1 Tbsp. Roux, (pg 208)

Preparations:

Sauté onions, green peppers in a sauté pan under medium heat until soft. Do not brown just sweat it. Add garbanzo beans, shrimps, potatoes, tomatoes sauce, black pepper, salt, thyme, cumin, ginger, onion powder, cinnamon, paprika, and water. Stir and combine well. Simmer and covered over low heat until gumbo has thickened. Add okra and check frequently to make sure stew is not sticking to the bottom for 10 minutes. Adjust seasoning if needed. Serve hot

Tip: This recipe pairs very well with and serve over brown rice.

Healthy Challenge for
ONE Day

Breakfast

1ea. English muffin, (no butter)

2oz.Turkey Bacon

1/2c. Black berries

Snack

1ea. Medium Banana or

1ea. Medium Apple

Lunch

2oz. Tuna, (in water)

1ea. Medium Pear

6ea Crackers, (no salt)

Supper

3oz. Veggie Burger

2ea. Slices of bread, (whole wheat)

1c. Spinach

Snack

1c. Carrot sticks

Tips: Drink plenty of Water-Water is quite simply the most important substance that a person needs in their diet on a day-to-day basis. It known to be as the building body block of life.

Notes

BREADS

- Mama's Homemade corn bread
- Johnny Cakes
- Buttermilk Biscuits
- Sweet potato bread
- Herds Parley rolls
- Cheese garlic biscuits
- Honey Wheat biscuits
- Naan bread

Note: A thick drop batter is (2 parts flour to 1 part liquid) and you can soften yeast in warm water.

Notes

Mama's homemade corn bread

Ingredients:

3 tsp. Butter

1/8 tsp Canola oil, (if needed)

1 Tbsp. Sugar

1ea. Egg

1Tbsp. Buttermilk, (add more if needed)

1/8 tsp. Baking powder

1/8 tsp. Baking soda

1/4c. Cornmeal

2Tbsp. All-purpose flour

Pinch. Salt

Pam Spray

Preparations:

Preheat oven to 375 F.

Spray Pam or use canola oil in a square or round pan. Melt butter in skillet and remove from heat. Mix dry ingredients; stir in egg, and buttermilk; pour in butter mix well, if any lumps mix for a few more minutes until batter is smooth. Pour batter into the prepared pan. Bake in the preheated oven for 30 to 40 minutes; or

until brown and firm; or toothpick inserted in the
center comes out clean. Serve warm

*Tip: This recipe pairs very well with scotch
bonnet mixed into the cornbread, or Jalapenos,
(chopped and seeded), or cream corn, cheddar
cheese and you got Mexican corn bread.*

Johnny Cakes

Ingredients:

1/2c. Cornmeal, (yellow or white)

1tsp. All-purposes flour

Pinch. Salt

1/4 tsp. Sugar

1/8 tsp. Vanilla extract

Pinch. Baking powder

1/2 Tbsp. Canola oil, (use more if needed)

¼ c. milk, (boiling, and low fat)

1ea. Egg

Pam Spray

Preparations:

Preheat oven to 350 degrees F

Lightly grease or spray Pam in a cake-baking pan. Sift cornmeal, salt, and flour together in a bowl. Then add milk and egg and mix well. Add sugar and baking powder and mix again. Then Pour in canola oil until it is all blend together. Pour mixture in b the greased cakebaking pan and bake for 20- 25 minutes or until golden brown. Cut and serve hot or room temperature.

Tip: this recipe pairs very well with syrup, or honey

Buttermilk Biscuits

Ingredients:

1/2c. All-purpose flour, (sifted)

Pinch. Salt

1/2 tsp. Vegetable shorting

1⁄8 tsp. Baking soda

1/8 tsp. Baking powder

1 tsp. Grated cold butter

1Tbsp. Buttermilk, (use a little more if needed)

1 Tbsp. Sugar

Pam Spray

Preparations:

 Preheat your oven to 375°F.

Spray counter with Pam before putting flour down on the counter. In a bowl, sift flour, salt, baking powder, and baking soda. Grate the butter into flour mixture; mix well. Add buttermilk; stir until dough leaves the side of bowl. Add a little flour on top of dough and counter, pat dough down; fold each side; gently pat again (do NOT roll with a rolling pin) Fold the dough about 5 times, gently press the dough down and make sure it is thick. Use a round cutter to cut into rounds or a glass jar. Gently knead the scraps together and make a few more.

Place the biscuits on a cookie sheet pan on the flour sides, do not let them touching each other, placed them about 1 inch apart. Bake for about 10-12 minutes; the biscuits will be a beautiful light golden brown on top and bottom. Serve hot

Tip: If you do not have a biscuit cutter, use a water glass or jar....This recipe pairs very well with jelly, syrup, or orange marmalade

Sweet Potato bread

Ingredients:

4oz. Sweet potatoes, (canned)

1Tbsp. Sugar

1ea. Eggs

1/8 tsp. Canola oil

1 Tbsp. Orange juice

1/2c. All-purpose flour

Pinch. Salt

1/8 tsp. Baking soda

1/8 tsp. Ground cinnamon

Pinch. Ground nutmeg

Pinch. Ground allspice

Pinch. Ground cloves

Pam Spray

Preparations:

Preheat oven to 350 degrees F.

Greased bread pan with oil or Pam

In a bowl, mash sweet potatoes; add sugar, eggs and oil. Stir in orange juice and mix. In a separate bowl, mix together flour, salt, baking soda, cinnamon, nutmeg, allspice and cloves. Stir flour mixture with sweet potato mixture until combine well. *Fold in pecans if desired*. Pour batter into prepared pans.

Bake until golden brown and stick a toothpick into center of a loaf to make sure it comes out clean. Serve warm.

Notes: These recipes measured for one service, but you can convert any amount of service if you like. Example; if you want to cook this recipe for 2, 3, or 4 people. The only thing you have to do is convert the amount into double, triple, or quadruple. If the original recipe call for ½ cup of flour and you cooking for two. Then you will use 1cup of flour

Herbs Parsley Rolls

Ingredients:

1/8 tsp. Yeast, (dry)

Drops of warm water, (for the yeast to dissolves, use more if needed)

Pinch. Sage

1/8 tsp. Canola oil

1/8 tsp. Thyme, (dried)

Pinch. Basil, (dry)

1/4 tsp. Parsley, (dry)

1/8tsp. Ground nutmeg

1Tbsp. Sugar

Pinch. Salt

1 egg

1Tbsp. Butter, (grated and cold)

1/2c. All-purpose flour, (divided it)

Pam Spray

Preparations:

Preheat oven to 375 F

In a bowl, dissolve the yeast in warm water. Add the sage, nutmeg, thyme, parsley, basil, sugar, salt, egg, butter or *margarine* in ½ of the flour. Using a wire whip, and whisk until smooth. Stir in the other ½ of flour with a wooden spoon and beat until smooth. Cover with a damp cloth and let rise in a warm place until doubled in volume.

Deflate batter by Stirring with a wooden spoon. Lightly grease or spray Pam in muffin pan. Drop 1 TBSP mound of batter into the prepared muffin pan. Fill each cup slightly more than 1/2 full; set aside in a warm place and let rise until doubled. Bake in the preheated oven until golden. Serve warm.

Cheese Garlic Biscuits

Ingredients:

½ c. All-purpose flour

1/8 tsp. Canola oil

1/8 tsp. Baking powder

1/8 tsp. Baking soda

Pinch. Salt

1/4 tsp. Thyme

Pinch. Ground black pepper

2 Tbsp. Butter, (1Tbsp. frozen and grated, 1 Tbsp. melted)

1tsp. Blue cheese dressing

1 Cloves garlic, (minced)

1 tsp. Ground garlic powder

1 Tbsp. Buttermilk

1 tsp. Parmesan cheese

Pam Spray

Preparations:

 Preheat oven to 375 F degree.

Grease or spray Pam on a baking sheet pan; in a bowl add flour, baking powder, baking soda, salt, thyme and black pepper together; mix well; add grated butter into the flour mixture until the result resembles crumbs; Add parmesan cheese, blue cheese dressing, and garlic. Make a well in the center of the flour mixture. Pour buttermilk into the well and fold with your hands until the dry ingredients just moistened. *If too moist, add a little more flour* Drop 1 TBSP mound of mixture, 2 inches apart onto prepared baking sheet pan.

Bake until lightly browned. Mix melted butter and garlic powder together. Brush biscuits with melted butter mixture. Switch oven to broiler, heat biscuits under the broiler until the tops browns. *Wait* until biscuits cool down before serving. Serve warm.

Honey Wheat Biscuits

Ingredients:

1/4c. Bread flour

1/4c. Whole-wheat flour

1 Tbsp. Honey

1/8 tsp. baking powder

1/8 tsp. Baking soda

Pinch. Salt

1 Tbsp. butter, (cold and grated)

1Tbsp. buttermilk, (use a little more if needed)

1 Tbsp. Sugar

Preparations:

Preheat oven to 375 degrees F

Mix the all-purpose flour, whole-wheat flour, baking powder, baking soda, honey, sugar, and salt in bowl. Add in grated butter and mix until mixture resembles coarse crumbs; stir in buttermilk until just moistened. Add a little flour on top of dough and counter, pat dough down; fold each side; gently pat again (do NOT roll with a rolling pin) Fold the dough about 5 -8 times, gently press the dough down and make sure it is thick.

Use a round cutter to cut into rounds or a glass jar. Gently knead the scraps together and make a few more.

Place the biscuits on a cookie sheet pan on the flour sides, do not let them touching each other, placed them about 1 inch apart. Bake for about 10-12 minutes; the biscuits will be a beautiful light golden brown on top and bottom. Serve hot.

Naan Bread

Ingredients:

1/8 tsp. Yeast, (dry)

2 drops. Warm water, (used for yeasts)

1Tbsp. sugar

1 Tbsp. Milk

1ea. Egg

Pinch. Salt

1/2c. Bread flour

1/4 tsp. Clove garlic (minces, optional)

1tsp. Butter, (melted)

Preparations:

Preheat a grill to high, after you make the dough.

In a bowl, dissolve yeast in warm water. Stir in sugar, milk, egg, salt, and ½ of flour to make a soft dough. Knead for 5 to 8 minutes. Spray counter, lightly floured surface until smooth. Place dough in a well-oiled bowl, cover with a damp cloth, and set aside to rise. Let it rise until the dough has doubled in volume.

Punch down dough, and knead in garlic, (optional). Pinch off small handfuls of dough about the size of a golf ball. Roll into balls, and place on a tray. Cover with a towel, and allow rising until doubled in size about 20 minutes.

Roll one ball of dough out into a thin circle. Lightly butter both sides. Place dough on grill, cook until puffy and lightly browned, and turn over. Grilled cooked side again and cook until browned, another 2 to 4 minutes. Remove from grill, and continue the process until all the naan has been prepared. Serve hot

Notes: These recipes measured for one service, but you can convert any amount of service if you like. Example; if you want to cook this recipe for 2, 3, or 4 people. The only thing you have to do is convert the amount into double, triple, or quadruple. If the original recipe call for ½ cup of flour and you cooking *for two. Then you will use 1cup of flour*

- Jerk Seasoning/ Sauce
- Eleven Herbs & Spices
- BBQ Seasoning
- Moroccan Seasoning
- Cacciatore Sauce
- Creamy Garlic Sauce
- Cucumber dressing
- Soy Ginger Dressing
- Pesto Sauce
- Roux
- Beef Consommé
- Veloute sauce
- Hollandaise sauce
- Tomatoes sauce
- Béchamel sauce
- Espagnole sauce
- White Stock
- Barbeque Sauce
- Honey Mustard Sauce
- Hot Dog Onion Sauce
- Lulu's special sauce
- Butter Sauce
- Vinaigrette Dressing

Tip: **The Using of the five Mother's Sauces**

- Béchamel-vegetables, pasta, eggs, fish, poultry, shellfish

- Veloute-Poached fish, lobster, white fish, crab, eggs, oysters, sweetbreads poultry
- Espagnole-grilled or sautéed meats and poultry, pork, broiled meats
- Hollandaise-grilled or sautéed meats and fish, eggs, poached fish, vegetables
- Tomato Sauce-Standard tomato sauce dishes— think spaghetti and pizza

Jerk Seasoning Sauce

Ingredients:

1/4 tsp. Garlic (Clove)

1/4 tsp. Ground allspice

1/4 tsp. Brown sugar

Pinch. Ground sage

1/2 tsp. Cayenne pepper

1/2 ea. Scotch bonnet peppers, (minced)

1/2 tsp. Ground thyme

1 ea. Green onions, (scallions chopped)

Pinch. Ground cinnamon

1/4 tsp. White vinegar

1/4 tsp. Orange juice

Pinch. Ground nutmeg

1/4 tsp. Salt

1 tsp. Black pepper

2 tsp. Gravy master, (Brown)

1 Tbsp. Canola oil

Preparation:

Combine all ingredients in a food processor or blender to liquefy. Pour Jerk sauce in a Jar and keep refrigerated. The sauce will hold good if kept refrigerated.

Tip: If you like to super-size the HEAT into the sauce, blend in some Trinidad moruga (Warning: Very Hot), or pot primo peppers or Jessie's Hot Pepper Dust (Warning: Very Hot) at any time. Just be careful with the heat.

Safety Note: Make sure to wear gloves when handling these HOT PEPPERS.

Notes: These recipes measured for one service, but you can convert any amount of service if you like. Example; if you want to cook this recipe for 2, 3, or 4 people. The only thing you have to do is convert the amount into double, triple, or quadruple. If the original recipe call for ½ cup of flour and you cooking for two. Then you will use 1cup of flour

Eleven Herbs and Spices

Ingredients:

1/2 Tbsp. Black pepper

Pinch. Salt

Pinch. Basil

1/8 tsp. Sazon, (con azafrin)

1 tsp. Garlic powder

1/8 tsp. Ground ginger

1⁄4 tsp. Onion powder

Pinch. Poultry seasoning

Pinch. Ground old bay

1/8 tsp. Parsley, (dried)

Pinch. Thyme, (dried)

Preparation:

In a bowl, combine all herbs, spices together, and use as need. Place in a jar or plastic container for storage away. Keep in dry place.

Tip: You can make a rub by adding a little stock until it becomes a paste. The rub is best use for just about anything. Also, be used for crabs, crab cakes, crab dip, cocktail sauce, shrimps and any prawn food.

Barbecue Seasoning

Ingredients:

1/2 tsp. Smoked paprika

¼ tsp. Seasoned Salt

1/4 tsp. Black pepper

Pinch. Garlic powder

Pinch. Ground cumin

Pinch. Sweet paprika

¼ tsp. Ground cayenne pepper

¼ tsp. Onion powder

¼ tsp. Ground turmeric

Preparation:

In a bowl combine all Ingredients; Use for seasoning your chicken, seafood, pork, lamb and more. Marinate over night for great taste. Place in a jar or plastic bag to storages.

***Tip:* You can make a rub by adding a little stock until it becomes a paste. The rub is best use for just about anything.**

Moroccan Seasoning

Ingredients:

1/4 tsp. Powder clove

1/4 tsp. Cinnamon

1/2 tsp. Turmeric

1/2 tsp. Ground caraway seed

1/2 tsp. Black pepper

1/4 tsp. Ground coriander

1/4 tsp. Ground cumin

1/4 tsp. Chili powder

1/4 tsp. Brown sugar

1/4 tsp. Salt

Preparation:

In a bowl, combine all ingredients, to season your meats, Chicken, fish, beef, lamb, and pork. The seasoning will hold good if kept in a dry area. After seasoning your meat kept

Overnight refrigerated. Place in a jar or plastic bag for storage.

Tip: You can make a rub by adding a little stock until it becomes a paste. The rub is best use for just about anything.

Cacciatore Sauce

Ingredients:

3 ea. Heirloom tomatoes, (skinned peeled and diced)

1tsp. Clove garlic, (chopped)

1/8 tsp. Canola oil

½ stalk. Celery, (diced)

1tsp. Red Pepper, (washed and chopped))

1 tsp. Mushrooms (wash and chopped)

1tsp. Green Pepper, (washed and chopped)

1/8 tsp. Onion, (washed and chopped)

Pinch. Dry Oregano

Pinch. Rosemary

1tsp. Red wine

1/8 tsp. Black pepper

Pinch. Salt, (optional)

Preparations:

Blend all these ingredients. Place onions, green peppers, celery, red peppers, garlic, rosemary and mushrooms in a food processor. Blend until chopped finely. In a small pot, heat oil over medium heat; Add vegetables mixture, diced tomatoes, salt, black pepper, oregano; cover and cook until all seasoning have blended together; stir occasionally. Add wine and cook about 20 minutes on low heat. Best serve hot.

Tip: Add-in, This recipe is paired well with savory grilled chicken, meatball and spaghetti, lamb, beef, and sliced turkey.

Creamy Garlic Sauce

Ingredients:

1ea. Clove garlic, (finely minced)

1/2c.Buttermilk Ranch Dressing

1/2. Lemon, (squeeze juice)

1/8 tsp. Honey

1 Tbsp. Parmesan Cheese, (grated)

1/2 tsp. Garlic powder

Pinch. Black Pepper

Pinch. Salt

Preparation:

In a mixing bowl, combine buttermilk ranch dressing, lemon juice, garlic powder, parmesan cheese, salt, honey and black pepper. Serve chill.

Tip: **This recipe pairs very well with a crispy chicken sandwich, for dipping sauce.**

Cucumber dressing

Ingredients:

1 Tbsp. Mayonnaise

1 Tbsp. Plain yogurt

1 tsp. Cucumbers, (seeded and minced)

1/8 tsp. Onion, (minced)

Pinch. Thyme

Pinch. Salt

Pinch. Fresh Dill, (chopped)

1/8 tsp. Garlic powder

1/8 tsp. Mustard

Pinch. White Pepper

Preparations:

Place In a food processor yogurt, mayonnaise, cucumbers, onions, thyme, salt, dill, garlic powder, mustard and white pepper; mix until smooth. Pour dressing into a stainless steel/or any bowl and chill in the refrigerator at least 20 minutes before servicing. Serve cold or room temperature.

Tip: this recipes pair very well with falafel, hamburgers, Asian salad, crisp chicken

Soy Ginger Dressing

Ingredients:

1/4c. Soy sauce

1/8 tsp. Fresh ginger, (minced)

1/8 tsp. Garlic powder

Pinch. Black pepper

1 tsp. Honey

1 tsp. whipped cream cheese

Preparations:

In a food processor add whipped cream cheese, soy sauce, ginger, garlic powder, black pepper, and honey; mix well. Place in a bowl and cover. Chill in the refrigerator at least 20 minutes before servicing. Serve cold or room temperature.

Tip: Use as a marinade for chicken, a salad dressing or a sauce with cooked spaghetti topped with craisins, and mandarin slices to create a cold Asian style noodle salad.

Pesto Sauce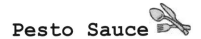

Ingredients:

2 tsp. Olive oil

1/2c. Fresh basil leaves

1ea.Clove Garlic, (chopped)

1tsp. Walnuts

1/2 tsp. Parmesan, (grated)

1/2 tsp. Romano, (grated)

Pinch. Salt

Pinch. Black pepper

Preparations:

In a food processor place basil, garlic and walnuts, slowly pour oil. Process until it is finely minced and smooth. Add both cheese, salt, and pepper. In addition, process very slowly; just long enough to mix well. Once ingredients are all combine, store in refrigerator to chill for 1 hour. Serve cold.

Notes: These recipes measured for one service, but you can convert any amount of service if you like. Example; if you want to cook this recipe for 2, 3, or 4 people. The only thing you have to do is convert the amount into double, triple, or quadruple. If the original recipe call

for ½ *cup* of flour and you cooking for two.
Then you will use 1cup of flour

Roux

Ingredients:

2oz. Butter, (or canola oil; bacon fat)

2oz. Flour

1/8 tsp. Salt

1/8 tsp. black pepper

Preparation:

You must cook the flour and fat together in equal
amount. Melt butter over low heat (do not brown).
Once the butter is hot enough, slowly whisk in the flour
and constantly about 3min or until it becomes thick,
rough paste.

*Tip: You can use the roux to make white, brown
gravy. Just add a little water until creamy.
Roux is a thickeners agent*

Beef Consommé

Ingredients:

1/8 Onion, (chopped finely)

1/8 Carrot, (chopped finely)

3/4 Egg whites

2oz. Lean beef

1/4 Celery, (stalks and chopped finely)

1/4ea. Roma tomato, (seeded and diced)

1c. Beef broth

Sachet:

1/2ea. Bay leaves

1/2ea. Sprig thyme, (fresh)

2 ea. Peppercorns, (whole)

1ea.Sprig Parsley, (fresh)

1ea. Cheesecloth (put the herds together in cheesecloth and tie it up)

Preparations:

In a stockpot place meat, onion, carrots, celery, and tomatoes and mix; Whip the egg white with a wire whip until frothy; add egg white to the meat mixture. Add the broth; mix well and add the sachet. Bring the mixture to a simmer over medium-high heat, stirring occasionally. Stop stirring once the raft begun to form. Break a hole in the center of the raft to allow the consommé to bubble through. Simmer over low heat until full flavor develops. Do not allow to boil, approximately 1hours. Strain through several layers of cheesecloth, degrease and adjust the seasonings if necessary. Serve immediately, or cool down and refrigerate.

Tip: This recipe is pairs very well for soups, soaking sliced beef.

Veloute Sauce

Ingredients:

1 Tbsp. Butter

1 Tbsp. Flour

1/2c. Chicken stock

Pinch. Salt

Pinch. White pepper

Preparations:

In a saucepan, heat butter over medium heat. Add the flour, salt and pepper. Cook to make a blond roux. Whisk in the stock to the roux until smooth, stirring constantly to prevent lumps. Bring to a boil; reduce heat low to a simmer about 10 minutes. Remove from heat and serve hot or warm. .

Hollandaise Sauce

Ingredients:

½Pot of water

2ea.Egg yolks

1½ tsp. Lemon juice, (whole lemon)

2Tbsp.Butter, (clarify, melted)

Pinch. Salt

Pinch. White pepper

Pinch. Cayenne pepper

Preparations:

Place pot on low heat until small bubbles, while what is at a simmer whisk egg yolks and lemon juice, white pepper, salt, and cayenne pepper together (best prepared in a stainless steel bowl), until it begin to thickened. Place the bowl over a double boiler of hot water. Do not touch the bottom of the bowl with the water. Continue to whisk rapidly. As the yolks cook, the mixture will thicken, be careful not to get the egg yolks to hot. Add the warm butter slowly to the egg yolk mixture a few drops at a time and continue to whisk until the sauce thicken. Pour mixture through cheesecloth if necessary to hold for service in a warm place. The sauce will hold for approximately 1 hours.

Serve immediately warm.

Tip: **This recipe pairs very well with egg benedict, French fries, turkey burgers.**

Tomatoes Sauce

Ingredients:

3ea. Roma tomatoes, (blanch)

1/8 tsp. Red wine vinegar

Pinch. Salt

Pinch. Black pepper

2 Tbsp. Onion, (chopped)

1/2 tsp. Clove garlic, (chopped

1 tsp. Fresh oregano, (finely chopped)

1 tsp. Fresh thyme, (finely chopped)

1/8 tsp. Fresh basil, (finely chopped)

1/8 tsp. Chive, (dried)

1/2 tsp. Parsley, (dried)

Ice water bath, (in bowl)

Preparations:

Heat up a pot of water until it comes to a boil. Also, set aside an ice water bath. Take the tomatoes and blanch the tomatoes to peel them: drop the tomatoes into the boiling water, until you see the skin starting to loosen and split, 10-15 seconds, lift the tomatoes out and put them into the ice water bath. After the tomatoes are cool transferring them from the ice water to bowl. Peels the skin from the tomatoes; chop the tomatoes then place in the food processor. Process until smooth for a pureed sauce. In a pot, bring the tomato sauce to a simmer over medium heat. Add black pepper, onion, garlic, oregano, thyme, basil, chive, and parsley and stir occasionally until the sauce reaches the taste and consistency you like. When finished cooking, stir in the red wine vinegar and salt. Add more lemon juice or vinegar to taste. Serve hot or cold

Cream Beurre Blanc Sauce

Ingredients:

4 Tbsp. Butter, (melted and clarified)

1 tsp. White wine

1/2c. Heavy cream

4 Tbsp. Butter, (softened)

1 tsp. Shallot, (chopped)

1/2 Bay leaf

1 Tbsp. Sugar

Pinch. Salt

Pinch. White pepper

Preparations:

In a saucepan on medium heat, place shallot, bay leaf, sugar, white pepper, and wine; and bring to a boil; reduce heat to low. Add the cream, and cook to a simmer, increase heat and simmer for 10 minutes. Remove from the heat and keep warm. Whisk the butter into the sauce until it has melted into the cream and thickened. You do not want the sauce to become too hot or too cold. Move the pan over the heat while stirring the sauce. Season the sauce with salt; strain if desired. Hold in a warm place. Serve hot.

Béchamel Sauce

Ingredients:

1c.Milk, (heated)

1Tbsp. Flour

5 tsp. Butter

1/8 tsp. Salt

1/4 tsp. White pepper

Pinch. Ground nutmeg

Preparations:

In a saucepan, heat butter on medium heat and simmer. Stir in flour and whisk constantly to prevent lumps and smooth or until it becomes thicken; paste like; add heated milk into butter mixture and whisk continuously until very smooth.

Reduce heat to low for sauce can simmer, add salt and pepper and continue cooking for 5minutes. Stir for 2-3 minutes or more. Remove from heat to prevent a skin from forming. Season nutmeg on top of mixture. Hold this sauce for later use, cool in an ice water bath. Serve warm or hot.

Notes: These recipes measured for one service, but you can convert any amount of service if

you like. Example; if you want to cook this recipe for 2, 3, or 4 people. The only thing you have to do is convert the amount into double, triple, or quadruple. If the original recipe call for ½ cup of flour and you cooking for two. Then you will use 1cup of flour

Espagnole (Brown Sauce)

Ingredients:

4 Tbsp. Butter

1 Tbsp. Onion, (chopped finely)

1Tbsp. Carrot, (chopped finely)

1ea. Celery, (stalks and chopped finely)

1/4c. Tomatoes sauce

3/4c. Beef broth

Roux, (pg. 206)

1/8 tsp. Salt

1/4 tsp. Black pepper

Sachet:

1/2ea. Bay leaves

1/2ea. Sprig thyme, (fresh)

2 ea. Peppercorns, (whole)

1ea.Sprig Parsley, (fresh)

1ea. Cheesecloth (put the herds together in cheesecloth and tie it up

Preparations:

In a stockpot, sauté the mirepoix (vegetables, carrots, onion, and celery) in butter until well caramelized. Add the roux. Add the beef broth and tomato puree, cook for

5 minutes. Stir to break up any lumps of roux. Bring mixture to a boil; reduce heat low and simmer. Add the sachet, and continues to simmer for approximately 1hour, allowing the sauce to reduce its sizes. Skim the surface as needed. Season black pepper, salt. Strain the sauce through a china cap with several layers of cheesecloth. Set aside; cool in ice water bath and hold for service. Serve hot or warm.

White Stock

Ingredients:

Bones:

3oz. veal

3oz. chicken

3oz. beef

Cold water

Mirepoix:

1 Tbsp. Onion, (chopped finely)

1Tbsp. Carrot, (chopped finely)

1Tbsp. Celery, (stalks and chopped finely)

Sachet:

1/2ea. Bay leaves

1/2ea. Sprig thyme, (fresh)

2 ea. Peppercorns, (whole)

1ea.Sprig Parsley, (fresh)

1ea. Cheesecloth (put the herds together in cheesecloth and tie it up)

Preparations:

In a stockpot, place bones and cover them with cold water, water must covered bones on high heat, bring water to a boil. Reduce heat and cover, and simmer for

4-5 hours skimming off the scum that rises to the surface. Drain off the water and the impurities. Again, fill the pot with cold water and bring to a boil. Reduce to a simmer and skim the scum that forms. Add the mirepoix and sachet to the simmering stock. Continue simmering and skimming the stock for another 4-5 hours. Strain stock, discard the vegetables and bones, cool and refrigerate. Serve hot or warm

Barbeque Sauce

Ingredients:

1/2c. Ketchup

1Tbsp. Grape jelly, (melted)

1/4 tsp. Mayonnaise

1/8 tsp. Mustard

1/2 tsp. Worcestershire sauce

1Tbsp. Sugar, (brown)

1/8 tsp. Chili powder

1/8 tsp. Garlic powder

1/8 tsp. salt

 Pinch. Paprika

1 tsp. Hot sauce

Preparations:

In a saucepan, combine all the ingredients over low heat. Stir until the sauce began to boil, reduce heat to low and simmer for about 5 minutes, then remove the pan from heat, cover and allow cooling. Store in refrigerator. Serve cold or hot

Tip: **This recipe pairs very well with ribs, chicken, and any style burgers.**

Honey Mustard Sauce

Ingredients:

2 Tbsp. Honey

2 Tbsp. Mustard

4Tbsp. mayonnaise

Pinch. Cayenne pepper

1/8 tsp. Salt

Preparation:

Whisk together all ingredients in a bowl until it mix
well, then store in refrigerator. You can serve it room
temperature or cold

***Tip: This recipe pairs very well with chicken
strips and serve as a dipping sauce.***

Hot Dog Onion Sauce

Ingredients:

2tsp. Canola oil

1/8 tsp. Chili powder

1/8 tsp. Onion powder

1small onions, (Julianne)

Pinch. Black pepper

1/8 tsp. Brown sugar

Pinch. Salt

1/4c. Ketchup

1Tbsp.Water

Preparation:

In a skillet, heat the oil over medium heat; add the onions and sauté until golden brown; stir constantly to make sure it would not stick to bottom of the skillet. Mix in the ketchup, chili powder, onion powder, black pepper, brown sugar and salt. Pour in the water; stir and bring to a boil, reduce heat to low and simmer about 10 minutes. When done set aside. Serve hot or warm.

Tip: This recipe pairs very well with hotdogs, hamburgers, sausages and garnish on top of grits.

Lulu's Special Sauce

Ingredients:

2 Tbsp. Mayonnaise

1 tsp. Hot sweet Chili Sauce

1 tsp. Hot sauce

1/2 tsp. Relish

Pinch. White pepper

Pinch. Salt

Pinch. Paprika

Pinch. Thyme, (dried)

Preparations:

In a small bowl mix all ingredients and stir until it all blended. Set in the refrigerator to cool or serve room temperature.

Tip: *Lulu's special sauce can be used it on just about anything, Suggest use for dipping sauce.*

Notes: *These recipes measured for one service, but you can convert any amount of service if you like. Example; if you want to cook this recipe for 2, 3, or 4 people. The only thing you have to do is convert the amount into double, triple, or quadruple. If the original recipe call for ½ cup of flour and you cooking for two. Then you will use 1cup of flour*

Butter Sauce

Ingredients:

4Tbsp. Butter, (melted)

1 tsp. Lemon juice

Pinch Salt

1tsp. Hot sauce

1 Tbsp. Hot water

Preparations:

In a bowl combine lemon juice and hot sauce, whisk
and set aside. Melt the butter in a saucepan under low
heat. Slowly whisk in water into mixture and bring to a
low boil for 2 minutes, stir frequently. Now stir in
butter.

*Tip: egg yolk good to use, but for one serves
you need half of a small egg yolk. You also, can
add garlic.*

Vinaigrette Dressing

Ingredients:

1tsp. Garlic powder, (or clove garlic, minced)

1/4c. Apple cider vinegar

1 Tbsp. Worcestershire sauce

1 tsp. Syrup

1 tsp. Olive oil

Pinch. Salt

Pinch. Black pepper

1/8 tsp. Thyme, (dried)

Preparations:

In a bowl combine apple cider vinegar, syrup, Worcestershire sauce, olive oil, garlic, salt, black pepper, and thyme; whisk until everything blend together. Use right away. Serve room temperature.

Tip: **This recipe paired very well with salads.**

DESSERTS

- Coconut Pudding (Tembleque)
- Raspberries Pop Ices
- Rice pudding
- Bread Pudding
- Fruit Salad
- Jelly Donuts
- Lemon Bars
- Peach Cobbler
- Banana Pudding
- Chocolate cake
- Carrot cake
- Apple Sauce
- Lemon Meringue Pie
- Crème Brulee
- Chocolate Raisin Oatmeal Cookies
- Apple Turn over Pie
- Tulip Flat Cookies
- Carmel Candy

Notes

Coconut Pudding (tembleque)

Ingredients:

½ c. Coconut milk, (can)

¼ tsp. vanilla extract

1tsp. Raisins

1Tbsp. Sugar

Pinch. Salt, (just a pinch)

2 tsp. Cornstarch

1tsp. Water

Pinch. Cinnamon

1ea. 5oz. Ramekin

Preparation:

In a non-stick, saucepan combines coconut milk, sugar, and salt and blend until mixture is nice and smooth. For the starch, put it into a glass. Then pour in cold water and stir. Pour starch mixture into saucepan. Cook mixture over medium-low heat. Stir with a wooden spoon until thickened; then pour into 5oz. ramekin and refrigerator for 1-2 hour. Serve cool; topped with raisins and cinnamon topping.

Notes: These recipes measured for one service, but you can convert any amount of service if you like. Example; if you want to cook this recipe for 2, 3, or 4 people. The only thing you have to do is convert the amount into double, triple, or quadruple. If the original recipe call for ½ cup of flour and you cooking for two. Then you will use 1cup of flour.

Raspberries Pop Ices

Ingredients:

1c. Raspberries, (fresh or frozen)

¼ tsp. Lemon juice, (whole lemon)

1 Tbsp. sugar

Water, (hot)

Preparations:

Place ingredients in blender and puree. Strain over a pitcher. Divide among Popsicle mode. Insert ice-pop sticks. Freeze until firm. When ready to eat, dip bottom of mold into hot water. Remove and serve.

Rice pudding

Ingredients:

1c. Low-fat 1% milk, (heated)

1c. Water

½c. Basmati Rice, (uncooked white or brown)

3 Tbsp. Sugar, (white or brown)

Pinch. Salt

1 Tbsp. Raisin, (soak in hot water for 20 minutes)

½ tsp. Vanilla extract

1ea. Egg, (beaten)

1tsp. Heavy cream 2ea.

5oz. Ramekin

Pinch. Cinnamon

Pinch. Nutmeg

Preparations:

In a bowl of hot water set the raisin in for 20 minutes. Cook rice and salt in water in a saucepan on medium heat. Bring to a boil, stir it; lower heat and cover until rice half done. Check with a fork. Stir in saucepan of rice-heated milk, heavy cream, sugar, raisins and vanilla and nutmeg; stir well. Bring to a boil and lower the heat. Let simmer until rice is very soft. Stir often.

Pour in beaten egg slowly and stir until egg mix in well continue to cook for 1 minute. Take off the heat and Pour into a 5oz. ramekin; cover with plastic wrap and let cool for 2 hours. Serve warm or cold; sprinkle cinnamon on top.

Tip: **Make sure to set raisin in a bowl or cup of boiling hot water for 20 minutes before putting it into mixture.**

Bread Pudding

Ingredients:

5sl. Bread, (toasted, cut into cubes)

1/2 tsp. Sugar, (use more if needed)

1ea. Egg

¼ tsp. Baking powder

1/8 tsp. Vanilla extract

1/4 c. Milk

1Tbsp. Butter

Pinch. Ground cinnamon

Pinch. Ground nutmeg

1/2 tsp. Raisins, (soak in very hot water for 20 minutes before using to plump)

¼ tsp. Coconut, (optional)

2ea. 5oz Ramekin

Pam spray

Preparations:

Preheat oven up to 350°F.

Grease ramekin with butter or spray it with Pam set aside. Place slices of bread in the oven and toast on both sides. Drain raisins if plump and set aside. In a bowl, combine cubed bread, raisins, sugar, baking powder, cinnamon, nutmeg, egg, milk, and vanilla. Mix well (If it too dry add a little more milk to make it wet). In a 5oz. Ramekin, pour bread mixture and leave a little space from the top. Place in oven; bake for approximately 30 minutes or until it browns. Sever warm or cold

Tip: **Make sure to set raisin in a bowl or cup of boiling hot water for 20 minutes before putting it into mixture. This recipe pairs very well with hot sliced peaches.**

Safety Tips: **When using eggs, make sure to crack eggs in a separate bowl before putting it into mixture. It is a good way to keep out eggs shells**

Fruit Salad

Ingredients:

1 Tbsp. Watermelon, (use a 40oz scoop)

1Tbsp. Cantaloupe, (use a 40oz scoop)

1 Tbsp. Pineapple, (cubes)

1Tbsp. Honeydew, (use 40oz scoop)

1 Tbsp. Granny smith apple, (cubes)

1 Tbsp. Fresh strawberries, (cubes)

1 Tbsp. kiwi, (cubes)

1tsp. Sugar, (brown)

1tsp. Granola

Preparations:

In a bowl, combine all ingredients except the granola and mix well. Cover with clean wrap and chill in refrigerator for 1 hour; when ready to eat sprinkle granola on top and enjoy. Serve cold.

Jelly Donuts

Ingredients:

1Tbsp. Sugar

1 Tbsp. Buttermilk, (melted; cold)

1ea. Egg, (beaten)

¼ tsp. Yeast, (dry active yeast)

1c. Canola oil

1 Tbsp. Butter, (melted)

1c. Bread flour, (more for dusting)

Pinch. Salt

1/8 tsp. Baking soda

1/8 tsp. Baking powder

Pinch. Nutmeg

Pinch. Cinnamon

½ c. Raspberry jelly

1ea. Donut filling injector

1ea. Deep fryer

Preparations:

Use a deep fryer or frying pan. Heat oil medium high.

In one bowl, place flour, salt, nutmeg, baking powder, baking soda and yeast. In second bowl place buttermilk, eggs, and melted butter. Place all dry ingredients in a separate bowl; pour slowly into the wet ingredients and fold, mix by using your hands or a wooden spoon. So that all ingredients mixed well, use your hands to knead to make sure the ingredients are fully mixed.

Set the dough aside for 20 minutes. Spray counter or cutting board with Pam before sprinkling extra flour. Place dough on counter or cutting board and roll out to 1/2inch thick. With a biscuit cutter or jar, cut disks. Place donut easily in hot oil, frying pan or deep fryer with a slotted spatula. Fry on both side until golden brown. Remove from oil and place them on a brown paper towel. Cool donut; inject raspberry jelly in the center with the donuts with injector filler. In a different bowl, coat the donut with sugar or cinnamon; Serve while warm.

Safety Tips: When using eggs, make sure to crack eggs in a separate bowl before putting it into mixture. It is a good way to keep out eggs shells.

Notes: These recipes measured for one service, but you can convert any amount of service if you like. Example; if you want to cook this recipe for 2, 3, or 4 people. The only thing you

have to do is convert the amount into double,
triple, or quadruple. If the original recipe call
for ½ cup of flour and you cooking for two.
Then you will use 1cup of flour

Lemon Bars

Ingredients:

½ c. All-purpose flour, (divided)

¼ c. Powdered sugar

4Tbsp. Butter, (softened)

1ea. Egg

1Tbsp. Sugar

2Tbsp. Lemon juice, (in bottle or fresh squeezed lemons)

1/8 tsp. Baking powder

Preparations:

Preheat the oven to 375F. Grease a baking sheet pan

Make the crust: In a bowl place 4Tbsp. flour, butter and powdered sugar. Mix mixture with your hands until it began to crumbly. In a lightly grease pan, firmly press dough. Bake until lightly browned. Transfer to a rack to cool.

Filling: Whisk egg, sugar and lemon juice in a bowl. Also, mix in the remaining of 4Tbsp.flour and baking powder into egg mixture; pour the filling over crust and bake at 350F until it is set. Transfer; let cool completely in pan on a rack. Lift out of the pan, cut into pieces (bars) and sprinkle evenly with more powdered sugar.

Serve cool

Safety Tips: When using eggs, make sure to crack eggs in a separate bowl before putting it into mixture. It is a good way to keep out eggs shells

Peach Cobbler

Ingredient:

1Tbsp. Butter

4 Tbsp. Sugar, (divided)

3 Tbsp. All-purpose flour

1/8 tsp. Baking powder

Pinch. Cinnamon

1/4c. Milk

1/2 c. Peaches slices, (canned, divided, and set aside)

1ea. 5oz. ramekin

Preparations:

Preheat oven to 375F.

In a pot, add 4 Tbsp. peaches, sugar, and butter. Cook mixture until butter and sugar melts on low heat. Pour the mixture in a 5oz. ramekin; Sift dry ingredients and add both, milk into a bowl. Make sure mixture is loosen; pour into the peaches mixture; do not stir. Spoon the other 4 Tbsp. peaches and the syrup from the canned peaches on top of the mixture; sprinkle cinnamon. Bake in 375F degree until brown. To serve, scoop onto small bowl and serve with your choice, ice cream or whipped cream

Banana Pudding

Ingredients:

1 Tbsp. Sugar

2 tsp. Cornstarch

Pinch. Salt

½ c. Milk

1 tsp. Butter

1 tsp. Sweetened condensed milk, (canned)

1ea. Small egg yolk, (save the egg white)

½ tsp. Vanilla extract

1ea. Ripe bananas, (thinly sliced)

Vanilla wafers cookies, (use as many as needed)

2ea. Ramekin, (5oz)

Preparations:

Preheat the oven to 325 F.

Add sugar, cornstarch, and salt saucepan. Stir until blended; Add milks. Cook over medium heat, stir constantly until mixture thickens as a custard, about 57 minutes, then remove from heat. In a bowl whisk in egg yolk and hot custard mixture; stir in vanilla and butter. Cook again for 1-2 minutes. Remove from heat.

On the bottom of the ramekin lay enough waffle; layers of banana slices to cover the bottom of a ramekin, then cover the bananas pudding mixture, repeat layering, ending with pudding on top.

Place the egg white in blender. Beat the egg whites at high-speed mixer until it foam. Add the sugar, and sweet condense milk gradually; keep beating until fluffy peaks form. Spread this over the top of the pudding. Bake pudding at 325F until the meringue becomes light golden. Allow to cool and serve cool. Refrigerate unused portions.

Safety Tips: When using eggs, make sure to crack eggs in a separate bowl before putting it into mixture. It is a good way to keep out eggs shells

Chocolate cake

Ingredients:

2-1/2 Tbsp. Butter

2 tsp. Cocoa powder, (baking cocoa, sifted)

1/3 c. All-purpose flour, (sifted)

1/3 c. Sugar

1/8 tsp. Baking soda

Pinch. Salt

1-1/2 Tbsp. Milk, (low-fat)

1/8 tsp. Vanilla extract

1ea. Egg whites (or use 1whole eggs)

Frosting:

4Tbsp. Cream, (heavy)

1/8 tsp. Vanilla extract 2oz.

Chocolate pieces, (melted)

Preparations:

Preheat the oven to 375°F.

 Grease and dust a ramekin 5oz. or cake-baking pan and set aside. In a mixing bowl, place sifted flour, sugar, baking soda and salt and set aside. In a saucepan, melt butter; add cocoa and mix well, simmer for 5 minutes; pour into flour mixture and stir lightly. In another bowl beat the egg whites and vanilla until well combined; pour into flour mixture; beat on low speed until just combined. Transfer to prepared ramekin 5oz or cake baking pan. Bake for about 30-35 minutes or until cake tests done (watch closely, do not over bake!). Toothpick or a skewer stick can test the cake. When done set cake aside to cool.

Frosting: heat cream until hot on low heat in another pot (non-stick), pour cream over the chocolate pieces stir well. Place mixture into mixing bowl. Place into refrigerate to cool. When it have cool down. Add vanilla and mix in a mixer, until fluffy. Frost each layer of cake. Serve cool.

Safety Tips: When using eggs, make sure to crack eggs in a separate bowl before putting it into mixture. It is a good way to keep out eggs shells

Carrot cake

Ingredients:
4 Tbsp. Carrots, (raw finely shredded)

1 Tbsp. Sugar

½ c. All-purpose flour

1/8 tsp. baking soda

1/8 tsp. baking powder

Pinch. Salt

Pinch. Cinnamon

1 tsp. Canola oil

1ea. Egg

1tsp. Chopped walnuts

Icing:

1/2 Tbsp. Cream cheese, (soft and room temperature)

1Tbsp. Butter, (soft and room temperature)

1/8 tsp. Vanilla extract

5 Tbsp. Sugar, (powdered)

Preparations:

Preheat oven to 375F. Greased ramekin 6oz

In a mixing bowl, combine sugar, oil, and egg. In another bowl, sift flour, baking soda, salt, and cinnamon. Mix wet ingredients with dry ingredients;

fold in carrots and walnuts and stir well. Put in greased 5oz. ramekin Bake for 55-60 minutes. Test to see if done with a toothpick or skewer and Cool down.

Icing:

In a mixing bowl, place cream cheese, butter, vanilla, and powdered sugar. Beat on low speed until thoroughly blended. Place in the refrigerator to cool. Once cooled spread over cooled cake. Serve cool.

Safety Tips: When using eggs, make sure to crack eggs in a separate bowl before putting it into mixture. It is a good way to keep out eggs shells.

Apple Sauce

Ingredients:

2 tsp. Sugar

2ea. Golden delicious apples, (peeled, cored and diced)

2- ½ Tbsp. Apple juice

Pinch. Cinnamon

Pinch. Nutmeg

1tsp. Raisin, (soak in hot water for 20 minutes)

Preparations:

In a pot, place apples and apple juice; bring to a boil on medium heat. Lower heat and simmer until apples is soft. Stir in sugar and cook until it dissolves. Add cinnamon and nutmeg stir through. Pour in a food processor and blend until it puree. Leave to cool in a refrigerator. Serve warm or cold. Sprinkle more cinnamon on top when ready to serve.

Tip: Make sure to set raisin in a bowl or cup of boiling hot water for 20 minutes before putting it into mixture.

Lemon Meringue Pie

Ingredients:

1/2 c. Graham cracker, (crumbs)

2-ea. 9 oz. ramekin

Pam Spray

Lemon Filling:

1/2 pk. Lemon pie filling

¼ tsp. Lemon zest, (from lemon)

1 tsp. Lemon juice, (fresh from lemon)

4 Tbsp. Sugar

2 c. Water, (divided)

1 ea. Egg yolk

Meringue Topping:

¼ tsp. Cornstarch, (optional)

1/8 tsp. Salt

2 Tbsp. Sugar

31 ea. Egg, (whites)

Preparations:

Preheat oven to 350 F.

Prepare lemon pie filling: In a pot on low heat. Add mixture with egg, sugar, lemon zest and 1-3/4 cup of water. Stir constantly until it reaches a thickness. Then remove from heat and set aside. In a food processor add graham cracker, by pulsing a few times; make sure the graham crackers are finely crumbs. Spray bottom of ramekins with Pam and then pack the bottom with the crumbs graham crackers. Pour the lemon pudding into the ramekins then set aside.

In a metal bowl beat egg white with a wire whip or mixer. Add salt, gradually add lemon juice, sugar and beat until stiff but not dry. When the egg whites are fluffy spread meringue evenly over the top of lemon pudding, starting with the edges, and then the middle. Lifting with the back of the spoon. Bake at 350 for 15-20 minutes, checking occasionally to make sure it is browning. Cool completely in refrigerator before serving.

Safety Tips: When using eggs, make sure to crack eggs in a separate bowl before putting it into mixture. It is a good way to keep out eggs shells.

Notes: These recipes measured for one service, but you can convert any amount of service if you like. Example; if you want to cook this recipe for 2, 3, or 4 people. The only thing you have to do is convert the amount into double, triple, or quadruple. If the original recipe call for ½ cup of flour and you cooking for two.

Then you will use 1cup of flour.

Crème Brulee

Ingredients:

1ea. Egg yolk

1 Tbsp. Sugar

½ tsp. Brown sugar

Pinch. Cinnamon

2/3 c. Heavy cream

½ ea. Vanilla bean, (split lengthwise and scraped)

5oz. Ramekin

Preparations:

Preheat the oven to 300°F.

In a medium bowl, whisk the egg yolks, sugar and vanilla; pour mixture in a saucepan, cook the mixture over low heat; bring to a boil. Stir consistency, but do not burn. Remove from heat when done set aside; remove vanilla bean and throw away. Strain the custard and pour it into a 5oz. ramekin or a shallow gratin dishes.

Set the ramekins in a small baking dish and add enough hot water to the dish to reach halfway up the sides of the ramekins. Bake for about 30 minutes, or until done.

Stick a tooth pick to make sure it come out clean; Remove from oven and cool in an ice-water bath for 10 minutes. Refrigerate for 5 hours or overnight. Sprinkle brown sugar evenly over custard; turn the oven on to broiler or a cooking torch to a caramelized crust. Bring ramekin close as possible to the heat source, until the sugar melts, forming a caramelized crust. Serve immediately and sprinkle cinnamon on top.

Tip: Aluminum foil is good to use to keep custard moist. Add-in, you add chips of almonds on top, or whipped cream...

Safety Tips: When using eggs, make sure to crack eggs in a separate bowl before putting it into mixture. It is a good way to keep out eggs shells.

Chocolate Raisin Oatmeal Cookies

Ingredients:

¼ c. All-purpose flour

Pinch. Baking soda

Pinch. Baking powder

Pinch. Salt

2- ½ tsp. Oats, (rolled)

1 tsp. Butter, (softened)

1 tsp. sugar, (white)

1 tsp. sugar, (brown)

1ea. Egg

1/8 tsp. Vanilla extract

1 tsp. Chocolate chips

1 Tbsp. Pecans, (finely chopped)

¼ tsp. Craisin

1 tsp. Walnuts, (chopped finely)

¼ tsp. Raisins (soak in hot water for 20 minutes)

1 Tbsp. Milk (as needed)

Pam Spray

Preparations:

Preheat the oven to 350F. Greased baking sheet pan.

In a bowl, whisk the flour, baking powder, baking soda, salt, oats, and pecans together and set aside. In another bowl, combine, brown sugar, butter, white sugar and blend with a hand mixer on low, beat in the egg until creamy, increase speed to high and beat in vanilla until incorporated. Stir in the flour mixture into the creamed mixture until no flour is visible. Now add the chocolate, craisin, pecans, walnuts, and raisins; stir to incorporate.

Use a spoon and press against side of bowl, pulling up to level dough. Drop 3-inches apart onto baking sheet; sprayed with nonstick spray. Bake 9 minutes, or until golden brown. Turn the pan once for even baking. When done set the cooking on tray to cool before transferring to a plate to eat. Serve warm or cool.

Safety Tips: When using eggs, make sure to crack eggs in a separate bowl before putting it into mixture. It is a good way to keep out eggs shells

Tip: Make sure to set raisin in a bowl or cup of boiling hot water for 20 minutes before putting it into mixture.

Apple Turnovers

Ingredients:

1ea. Frozen puff Pastry, (defrosted)

1ea. Egg, (lightly beaten for wash)

1 tsp. Butter, (melted)

1-ea. Granny smith apples (peel and cored and sliced)

1tsp. sugar

1 Drop. Vanilla

Pinch. Ground cinnamon

Pinch. Ground nutmeg

Pinch. Salt

1 tsp. icing sugar, (for dusting)

Pam Spray

Preparations:

Preheat the oven to 380; Spray baking sheet pan.

In a saucepan melt butter over medium heat; cook apple; stirring occasionally until tender. Stir in sugar, nutmeg and cinnamon. Cook; stir until liquid boils and thickens. Transfer mixture to a bowl; set aside to cool, and then chill until mixture is cold. Cut each pastry sheet into 4 or 2 even sized squares. It depend on how big you want your apple turnover pies. Brush the edges of each pastry with egg wash; spoon 2 Tbsp. of apple mixture onto one-half of each pastry square.

Fold the pastry diagonally over the apple mixture and seal by pressing the edges with a fork. Transfer to the sheet pan; brush with remaining egg, make sure to make two slits in the center of the pies; Bake for 20 minutes or until golden brown. Dust with icing sugar and serve room temperature.

Safety Tips: When using eggs, make sure to crack eggs in a separate bowl before putting it into mixture. It is a good way to keep out eggs shells.

Notes: These recipes measured for one service, but you can convert any amount of service if you like. Example; if you want to cook this recipe for 2, 3, or 4 people. The only thing you have to do is convert the amount into double, triple, or quadruple. If the original recipe call for ½ cup of flour and you cooking for two. Then you will use 1cup of flour.

Tulip Flat Cookies

Ingredients:

1 tsp. Butter, (softened)

1ea. Egg, (white)

1/2 tsp. White sugar

1/2 tsp. Brown sugar

¼ tsp. Confectioners' sugar

1 Tbsp. All-purpose flour

1/8 tsp. Vanilla extract

Pam Spray

Preparations:

Preheat the oven to 350F

Line a baking sheet with parchment paper; Spray with Pam

In a bowl, mash butter, white sugar together with a fork until creamy; mix the flour, vanilla extract, and egg whites to make a loose smooth batter. Take a teaspoon and full it with batter, drop about 2 tsp of mixture onto the prepared baking sheet. Use the spoon to spread the dough out into a very thin circle. Repeat with the remaining batter.

Bake in the preheated oven until the cookies are light browned at the edges and the centers done, 5 to 8minutes. Make sure you do not over bake them. When cookies is done, immediately take cookies off tray and drape them over the greased glasses to mold them and harden into a small wavy bowls, or you leave them flat; sprinkle confectioners' sugar. Allow to cool completely. Serve cool

Safety Tips: When using eggs, make sure to crack eggs in a separate bowl before putting it into mixture. It is a good way to keep out eggs shells

Carmel candy

Ingredients:

4 ea. Carmel, (cube)

1/3 c. White sugar

1/3c. Brown sugar

1 Tbsp. Butter

1 Tbsp. Corn syrup

¼ c. Heavy cream

1/8 tsp. Vanilla

Pinch. Salt

1 Tbsp. Water Candy

Thermometer

Preparation:

Line a cookie sheet pan with foil. Pam spray the foil. Combine brown sugar, white sugar, water, butter, corn syrup, cream, and vanilla in a saucepan. Cook over medium heat, stirring constantly until mixture reaches it melted point. Remove the sugar mixture from heat and add butter. Stir constantly until butter and sugar mixture is blended. Then set aside. Take the mixture and pour onto the sheet pan and let sit until cool down for ½-1 hour for completely. Cut candy into square shapes and wrap in waxed paper.

Tip: Add-in, you can make caramel apples:
Wash the apple and dry it off. Stick- sticks into
the bottom of the apples. Take the apple, dip
the apples, and sit them on waxed paper, used
Pam spray.

Homemade Gifts

- Marinated Olives and Mushrooms
- Spicy **"Hot"** Pickled Cucumbers
- Flavored Seasoned Popcorn
- Cheese Sticks
- Orange Party Punch
- Fruity Raspberry Ices Tea
- Foot Bath
- Massage Oil
- Cook's Basket

Notes

Marinated Olives and Mushrooms

Ingredients:

8oz. Jar of Olives, (drained)

½ c. Mushroom, (fresh, any kind)

¾ tsp. Olive oil

1 ea. Garlic cloves, (sliced)

1 ea. Shallots, (minced)

½ tsp. Balsamic vinegar

1 ea. Sprigs thyme

¼ tsp. Fresh sage leaves, (chopped)

1 tsp. Fresh parsley, (chopped)

1 bay leaf

Pinch salt

½. Scotch bonnet peppers, (cut into rings)

Preparation:

Soak the mushrooms in boiling water for 10 minutes, and then drain them. Slice them into thick size pieces. Drained the jar of olives and put aside; Heat olive oil in a frying pan. Add mushrooms and sauté them over low heat until the mushrooms are sweating and brown, about 10 minutes. Transfer them into a bowl and allow cooling.

In a small saucepan with a little olive oil, simmer the garlic, shallots, olives and vinegar. Add all of the fresh herbs, and salt. Combine mushrooms, olives, peppers, and all ingredients into pan and cook until the mixture well mixed together, then pack everything in their liquid into jars, and allow them to cool. Store jar in the refrigerator for about 2 days - 1 week before eating them. They need time to marinade for the flavors to develop. Bring the jar to room temperature before serving.

Tips: You can eat it with crusty bread and salad as a starter.

Spicy Hot Pickled Cucumbers

Ingredients:

1ea. Cucumbers, (sliced thin)

½ tsp. Scotch bonnet, (slice thin, wear gloves while cutting pepper)

½. Fresh mint leaf

2 tsp. Wine vinegar

½ tsp. Sugar

¼ tsp. Dill seeds

1 sprig of fresh dill

1 tsp. picking spice

Pinch. Salt

Pinch. Parley, (dried)

Preparation:

Combine the cucumbers, vinegar; scotch bonnet, sugar, garlic, salt, pickling spice, dill seed in a bowl and let stand at room temperature for 5 hours, until the sugar and salt dissolve. Then put the cucumbers into a jar with the liquid. Place a sprig of fresh dill into jar, and seal with lids. Refrigerate for 10-15 days before eating.

Tips: WARNING! I recommend wearing gloves when you are working with hot peppers and thoroughly washing your hands, cutting boards and knives with hot soapy water after you have finished. Avoid touching your face and eyes.

Flavored Seasoned Popcorn

Ingredients:

1bg. Microwave popcorn (popped)

2 Tbsp. Butter, (melted)

Pinch. Black pepper

Pinch. Thyme, (dried)

Pinch. Dill, (dried)

Pinch. Ground parsley

Pinch. Smoked paprika

Pinch. Lawry's Seasoned Salt

Pinch. Garlic powder

Pinch. Cayenne pepper

Pinch. Onion powder

2 tsp. Cheddar cheese powder

Preparation:

In a large bowl, add popcorn, all the seasoning and Cheddar cheese powder. Toss until popcorn well coated, then pour melted butter over popcorn, tossing again to coat. You can serve immediately or wait until seasoning settle.

Tips: If you like it sweet and savory. Add-in, you can add M&Ms.

Cheese Sticks

Ingredients:

1 pieces string cheese

2 ea. Breadstick dough, (store bought)

½-1 tsp. Pesto sauce, (pg 204)

1sm egg white, lightly beaten

1tsp-grated Parmesan

½ c. Water

Pam Spray

Preparation:

Preheated oven to 380 F.

Greased a baking sheet pan with pam. Slice string cheese in half, the long way. Cut the breadstick dough into 2 strips. Then you spread some pesto sauce in the center of the dough. Place the string cheese half in the middle of the dough with pesto. Do the same to second strip of dough. Moisten edges with water, press down, and fold dough over cheese until dough is sealed. After the dough is sealed, twist it two times. Put breadsticks on greased baking sheet. Brush beaten egg white, then sprinkle grated Parmesan. Make three knives slash across the top of breadsticks. Bake until golden brown and puffed. Let cheese sticks cool slightly. Serve with warmed marinara sauce for dipping.

Orange Party Punch

Ingredient:

1/2c. Orange juice (concentrated)

1Tbsp Lemon Juice

2 Tbsp. Light rum

1/2c. Ginger ale

1 tsp. Mango, (diced)

1 tsp. Papaya, (diced)

1 tsp. Kiwi, (diced)

1 tsp. Pineapple, (diced)

Preparation:

Combine in a bowl, oranges, lemon juice, light rum, mango, papaya, kiwi, and pineapple and mix well. Chill for 3 hours. Pour in ginger ale just before serving.

Tips: **Alternatively, make fruit ice cubes using chunks of the same types of fruits or add more light rum....WARNING! This punch consumes ALCOLHOL**

Fruity Raspberry Ices Tea

Ingredients:

1 bag of tea (brew)

2 cups of water

2 Tbsp. Raspberry

1 Tbsp. Strawberries, (diced)

½ sl. Orange, (Cut into cubes)

1 sl. Pineapple, (cut into cubes)

1tsp. Blueberries

Preparation:

Boil 1 tea bag; put the tea to the side to cool off. After tea is Luke warm pour tea into a 16oz glass, add all the fruits, stir gently then set in the refrigerator until the tea is cold. Put ice into glass and full it up with the fruity tea.

Tips: This recipe pairs very well with sugar or honey.

Foot Bath

Ingredient:

2 Tbsp. Baking Soda

1 Pale warm water

10 drops Lavender oil

10 drops Baby oil

2 Tbsp. Chamomile, (herbal)

Preparation:

In the pale of water, spoon in baking soda, and chamomile. Add a few drops of lavender oil, and baby oil. Soak for 15-20 minutes and scrub with a washcloth gently. Follow with an application of a rich moisturizer and a warm towel to wrap your foot. Sit for 20 minutes. Feet will feel clean.

Massage Oil

Ingredients:

10 drops lavender oil

10 drops rosemary oil

10 drops begamont oil

10 drops Olive oil

Preparation:

Combine all oils in a bottle and shake well about
4mintues. Then pour a small amount into your hand.
Rub hands together and gently apply on body.

Cook's Basket

Ingredients:

1 ea. Large basket

1 ea. potholder

1 ea. Tonge

1 ea. Rolling pin

1ea. Cook's towel

1 pk. Wooden utensils

1ea. Apron

1 ea.-measuring spoon

1 ea. Can opener

1 ea. Cookbook

1 ea. Grater

1 ea. Spoon

1 ea. Fork

1 ea. Spatula

1 ea. Turner

1 Cello paper

1 ea. Ribbon

1ea. Bow

1 ea. Gift card

Preparation:

First, on a wide table spread out the clear cello roll, then set basket into the center. Decorate the bottom of the basket with Art Tissue Paper. Take all of the items and organize it into the basket. Bring the cello paper up to cover all the items until you make a ponytail, wrap the ribbon around and tie it tight, add bows and card.

Tips: **The basket may be a color scheme, the container, the arrangement, or the theme.**

<u>Introducing</u>

Jesse's death dust. Is a hot pepper flakes that is extremely, extremely, extremely hot. The ingredients of the peppers are the hottest pepper in the world the best example is the Carolina reaper. Warning make sure when using these products to wash your hands because the death dust can burn your eyes, please if purchase this item be cautious. If you like to purchase one email the person at the follow email:

<u>jesseCzy817@yahoo.com</u>

or

<u>shOgun187@yahoo.com</u>

Good luck and be cautious.

The author of this book, is not responsible for any purchase that is made from this product

Lulu's Index:

A

B

C

N

O